Kindergarten Math
with Confidence
Student Workbook

Kindergarten Math
with Confidence
Student Workbook

KATE SNOW

WELL-TRAINED MIND PRESS

Table of Contents

This Student Workbook is only one component of *Kindergarten Math with Confidence*, and it is not meant to be used as a stand-alone workbook. The hands-on teaching activities in the Instructor's Guide are an essential part of the program.

Trace.

Circle the 1s.

HIGHWAY 1

1:00

4317

$1.52

September 1, 2020

Trace.

Circle the pairs.

Trace.

Match.

Trace.

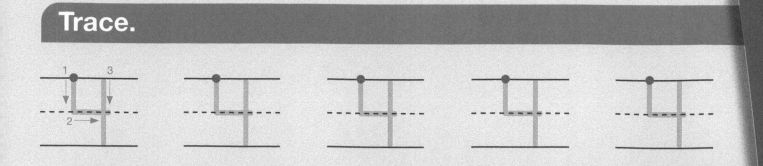

Draw 4 balls in each box.

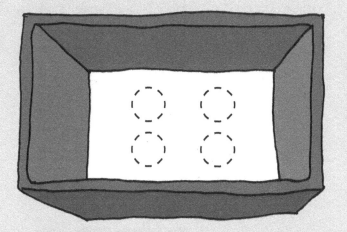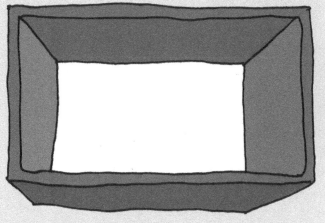

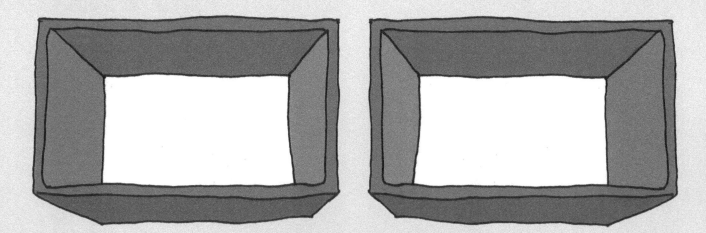

Trace.

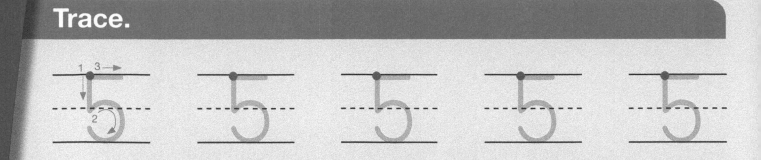

Match.

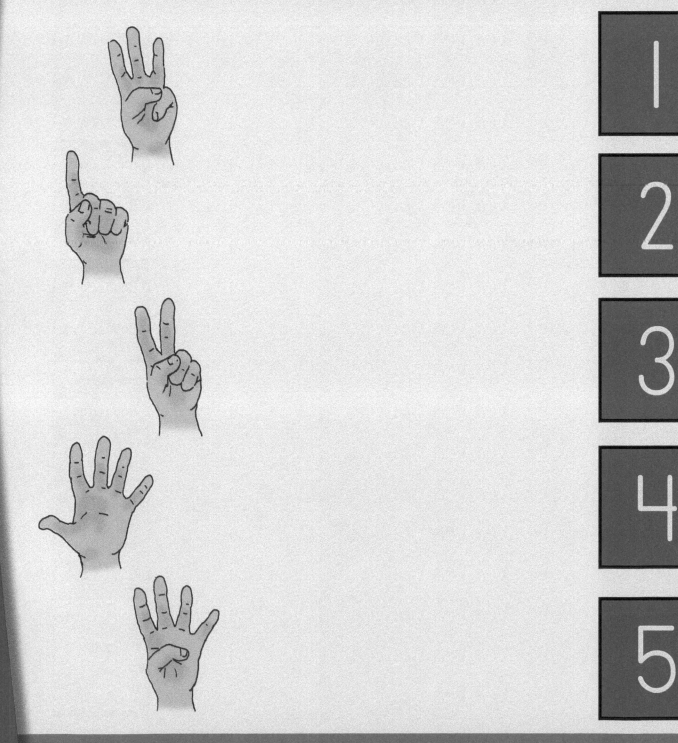

Trace.

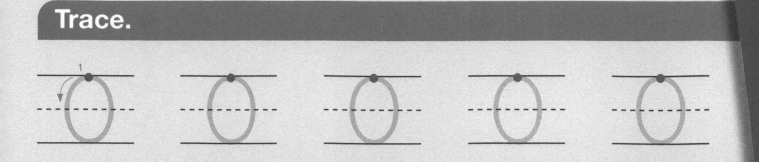

Match.

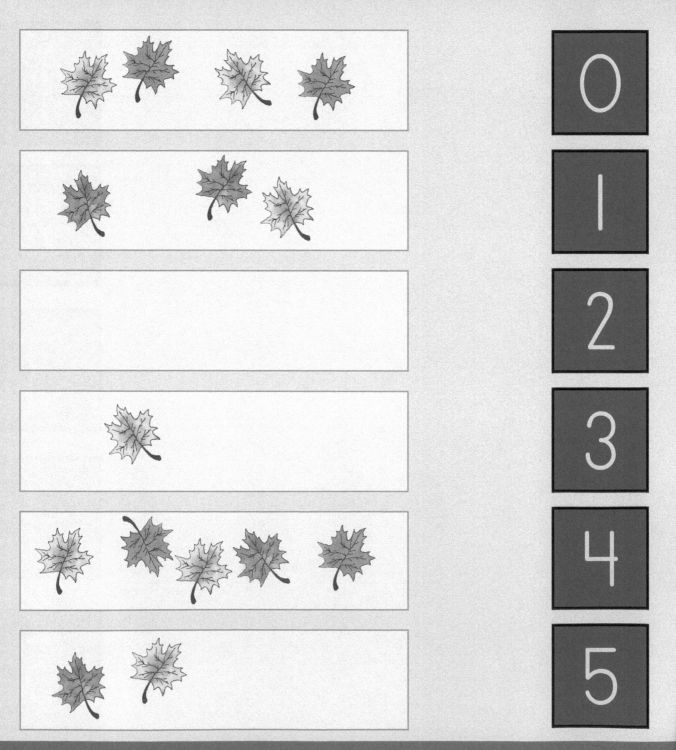

Trace.

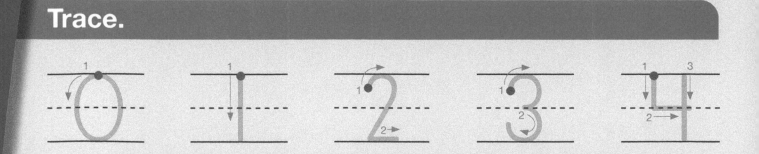

Draw circles to match.

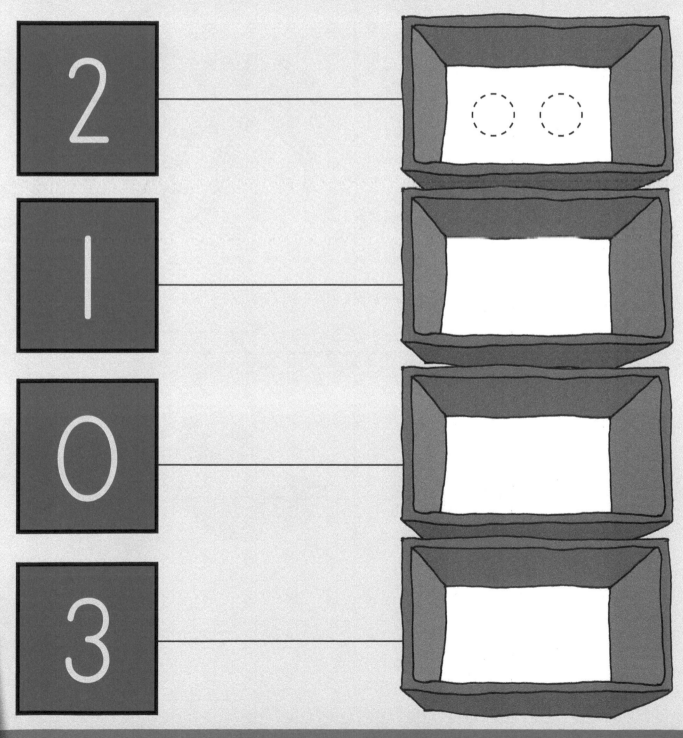

Write how many.

_____

- - - - - - - - -

_____

_____

- - - - - - - - -

_____

_____

- - - - - - - - -

_____

_____

- - - - - - - - -

_____

Trace.

Circle the groups of 6. X the other groups.

Trace.

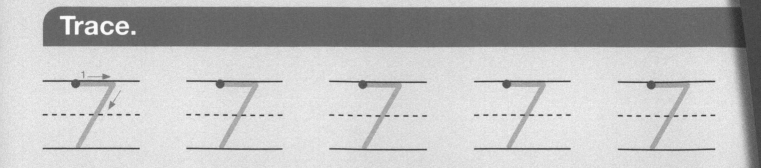

Draw circles to match.

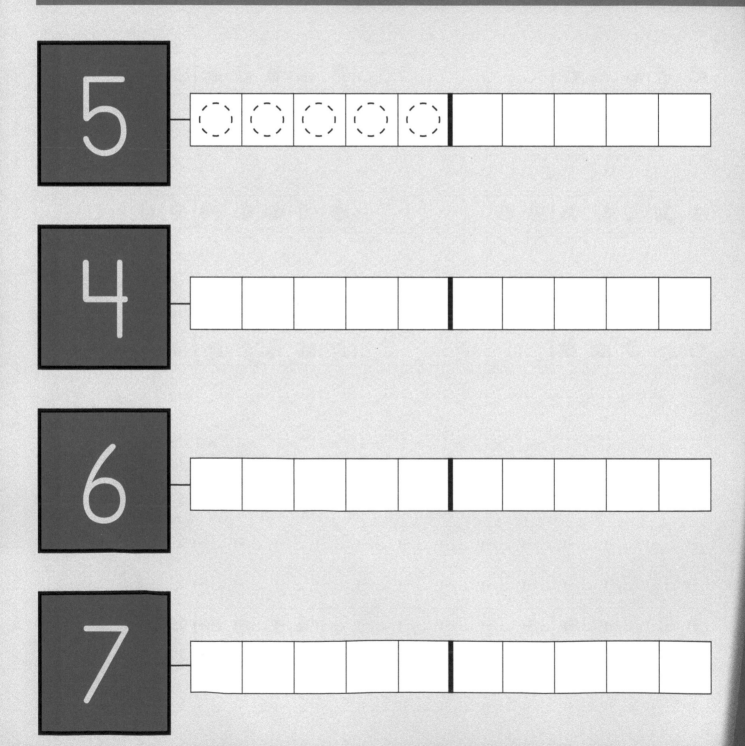

Trace.

8   8   8   8   8

Circle the groups of 8. X the other groups.

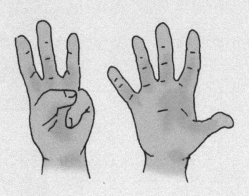
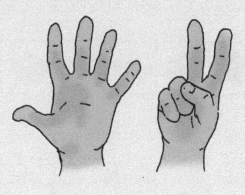

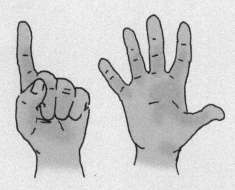
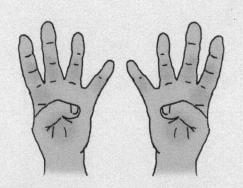

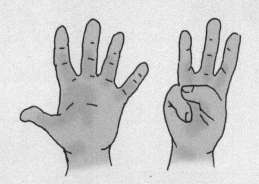
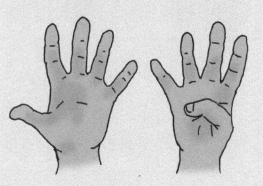

Trace.

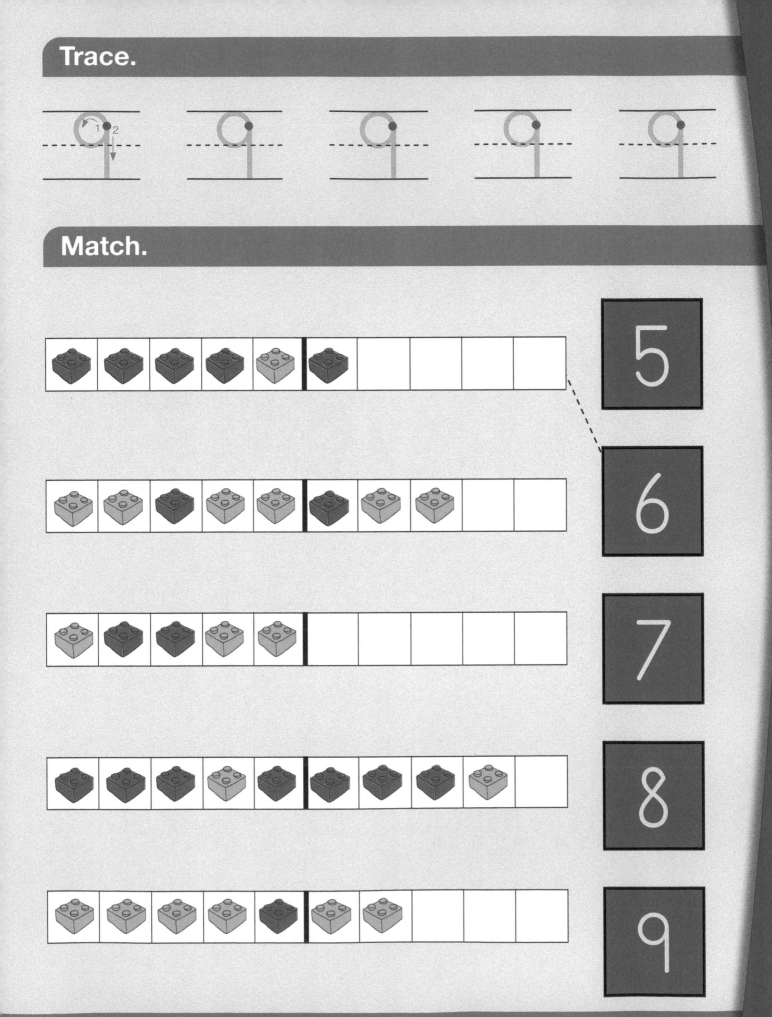

Match.

Trace.

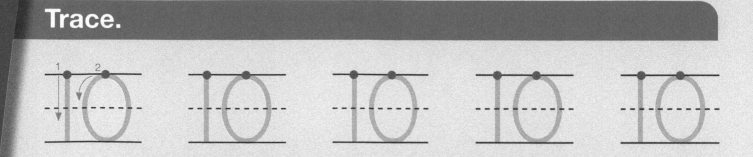

Connect the dots in order.

Trace.

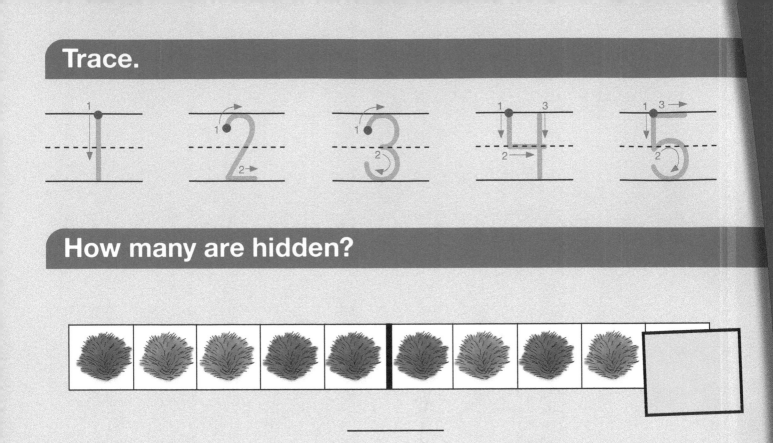

How many are hidden?

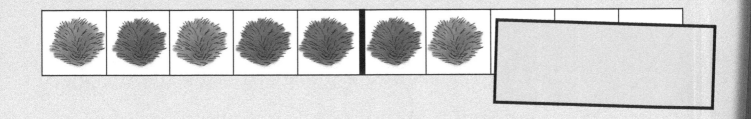

_____

- - - - - - - - - -

_____ are hidden.

_____

- - - - - - - - - -

_____ are hidden.

_____

- - - - - - - - - -

_____ are hidden.

Trace.

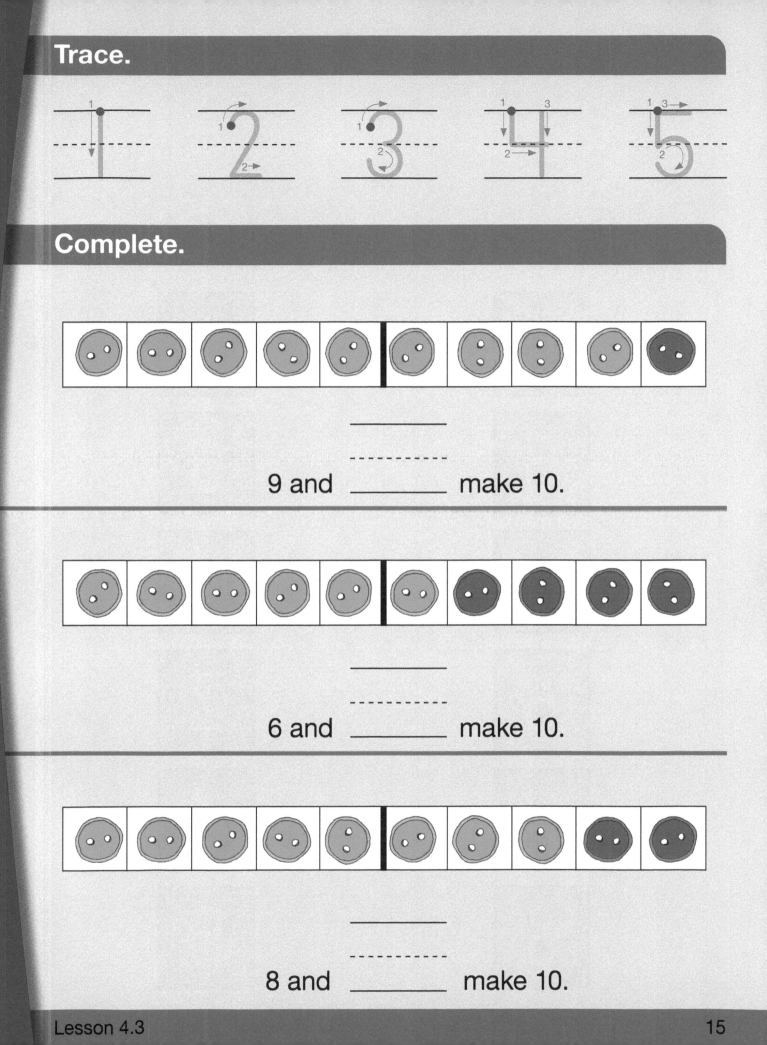

Complete.

9 and _____ make 10.

6 and _____ make 10.

8 and _____ make 10.

Trace.

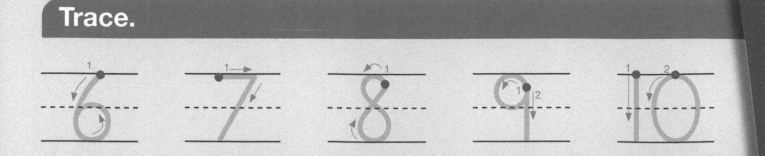

Match pairs that make 10.

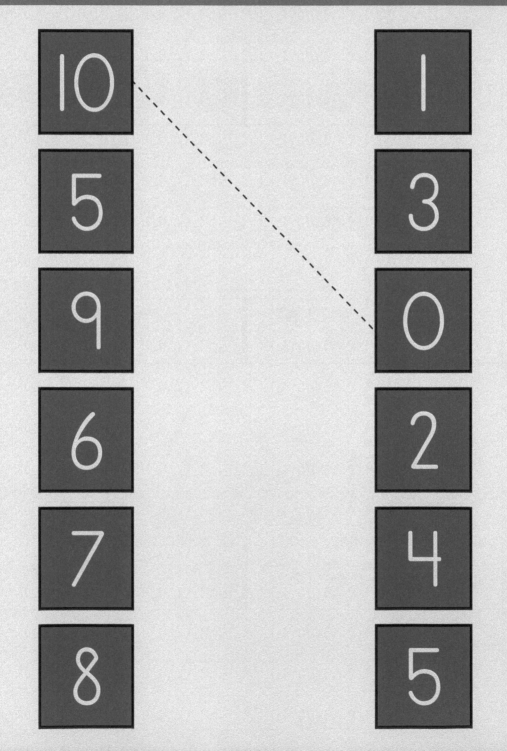

Trace.

6 7 8 9 10

X the one that doesn't belong.

Trace.

1   2   3   4   5

X the one that doesn't belong.

Trace.

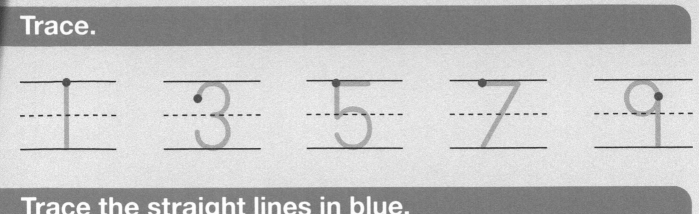

Trace the straight lines in blue.
Trace the curved lines in red.

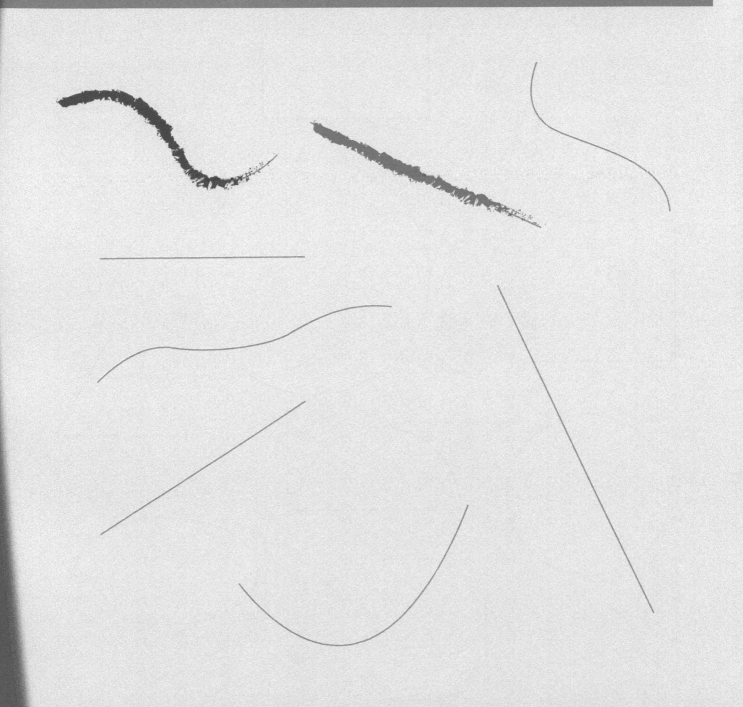

Trace.

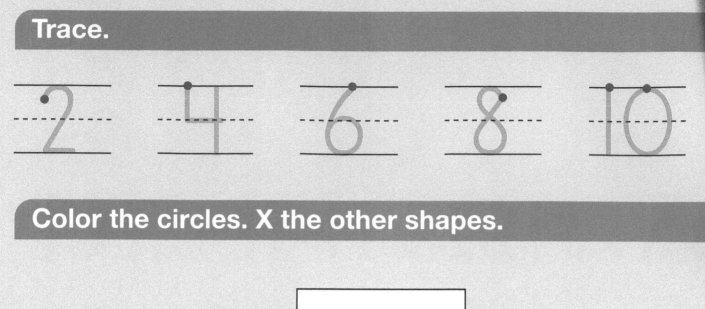

Color the circles. X the other shapes.

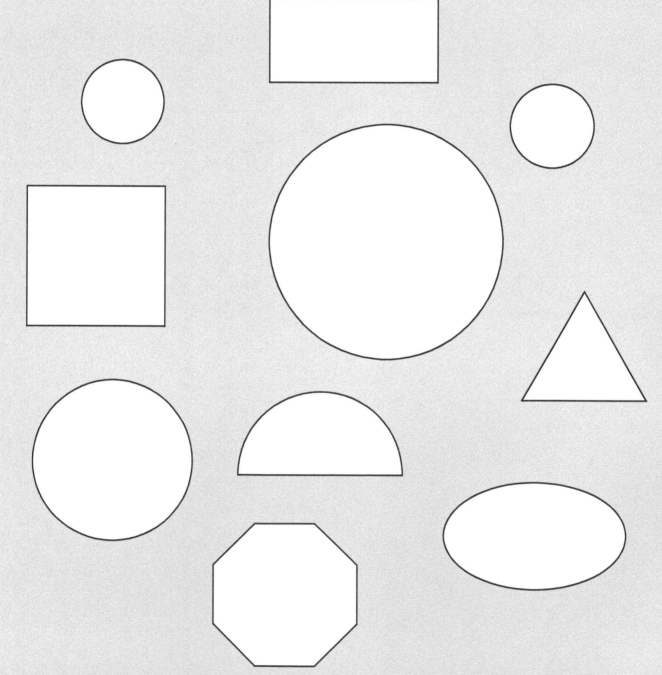

Trace.

2   3   4   5   6

How many sides?

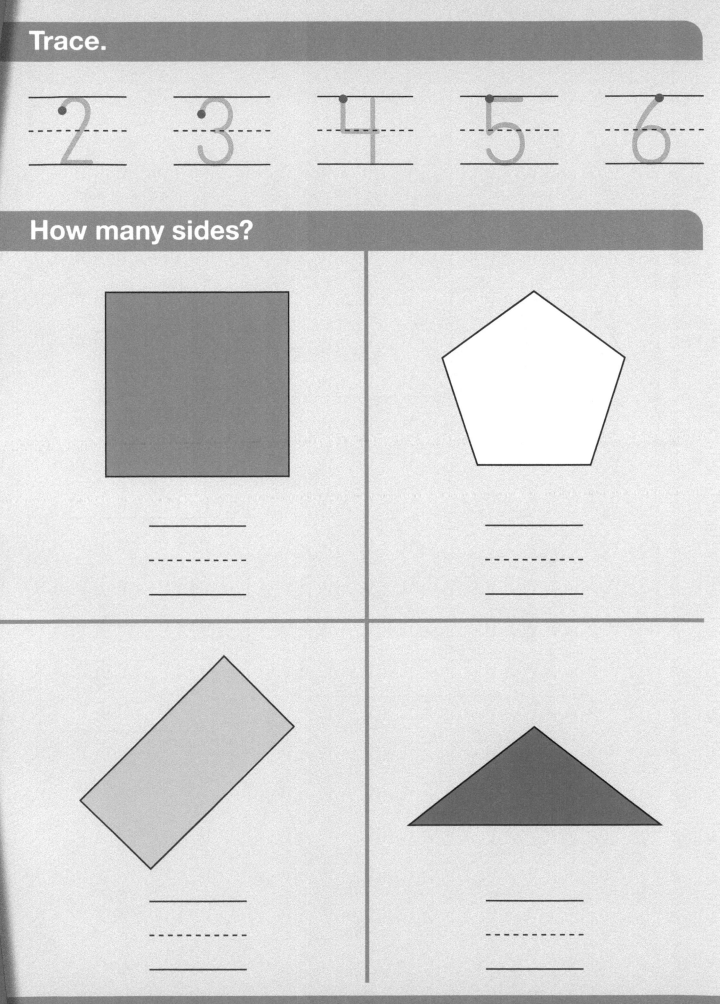

Trace.

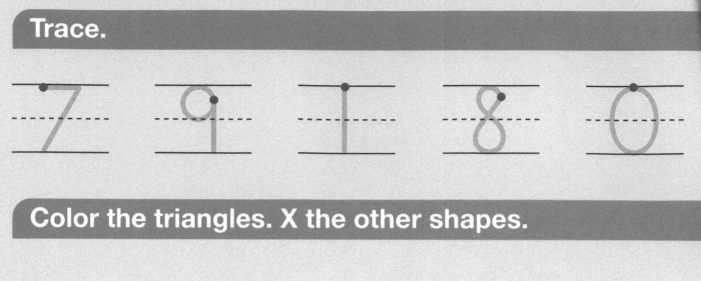

Color the triangles. X the other shapes.

Trace.

Color the rectangles in the picture.

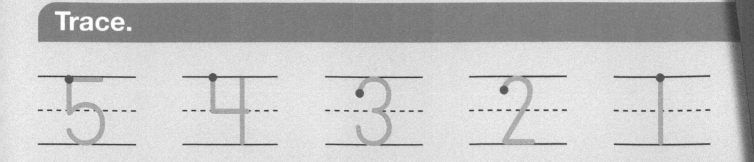

Color the squares. X the other shapes.

Trace.

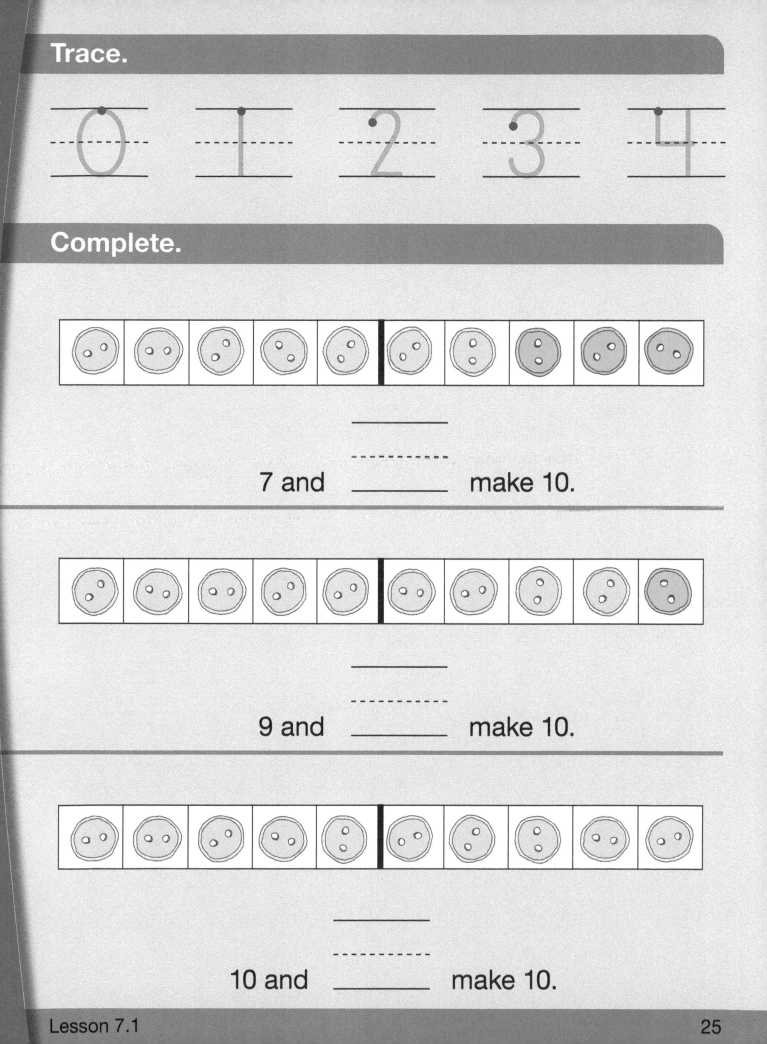

0 1 2 3 4

Complete.

_____

7 and _____ make 10.

_____

9 and _____ make 10.

_____

10 and _____ make 10.

Trace.

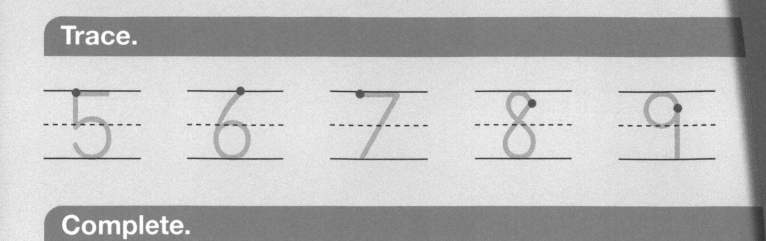

Complete.

_____
- - - - - - - - - - -
4 and _____ make 10.

_____
- - - - - - - - - - -
2 and _____ make 10.

_____
- - - - - - - - - - -
3 and _____ make 10.

Trace.

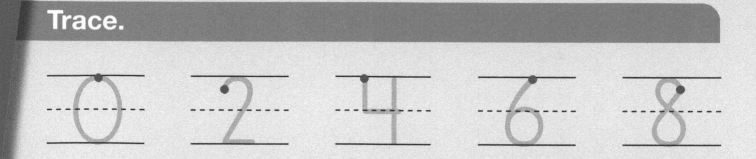

0   2   4   6   8

Use pattern blocks to cover each outline.

Trace.

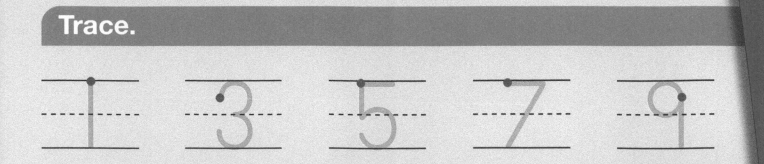

1 3 5 7 9

Use pattern blocks to cover the outline.

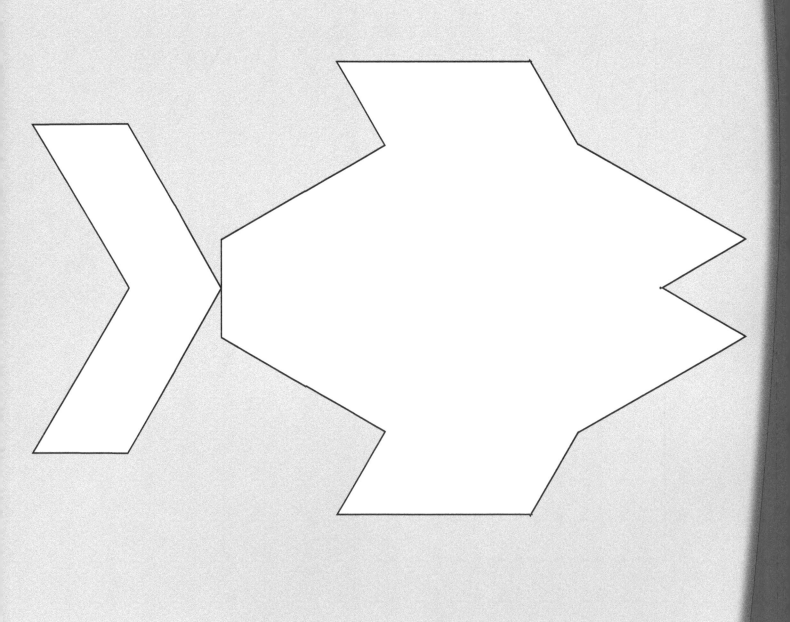

Trace.

Circle the symmetric shapes.
X the shapes that are not symmetric.

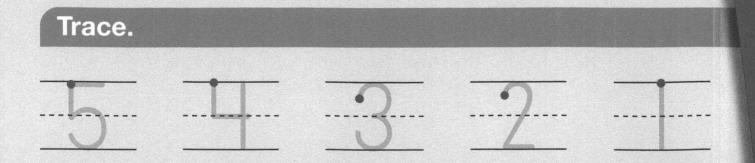

Use pattern blocks to finish the symmetric design.

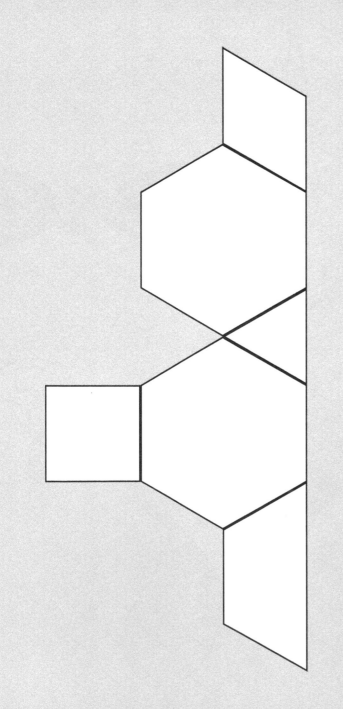

Trace.

Draw a symmetric picture of yourself.

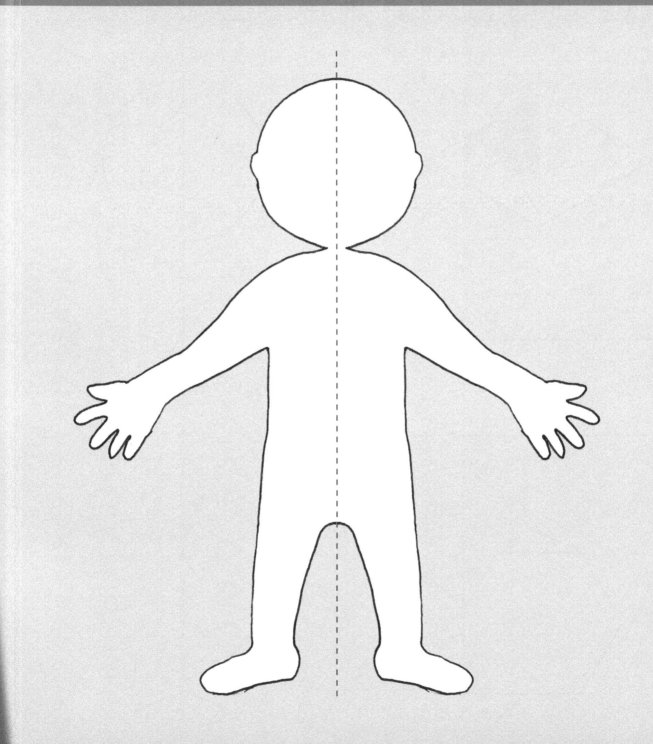

Trace.

Color the left side of each picture yellow.
Color the right side of each picture red.

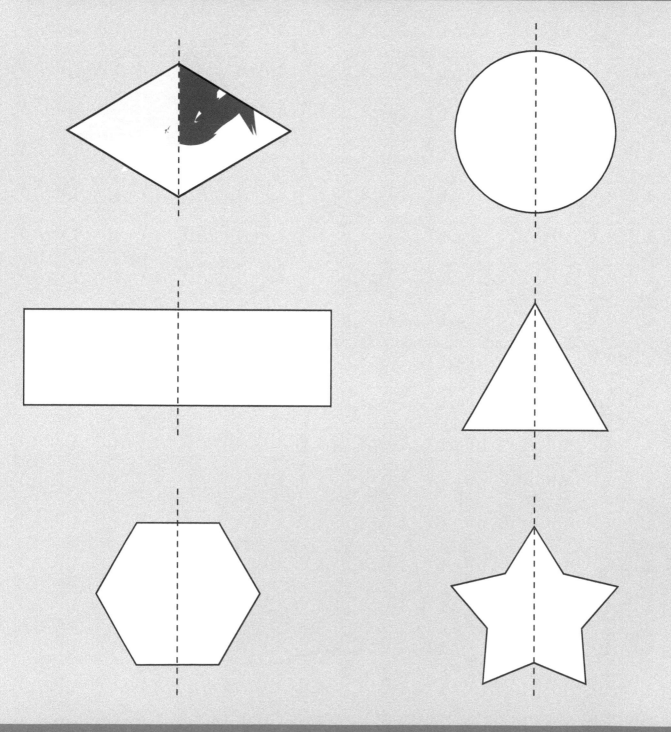

Trace.

1   2   3   4   5

Complete.

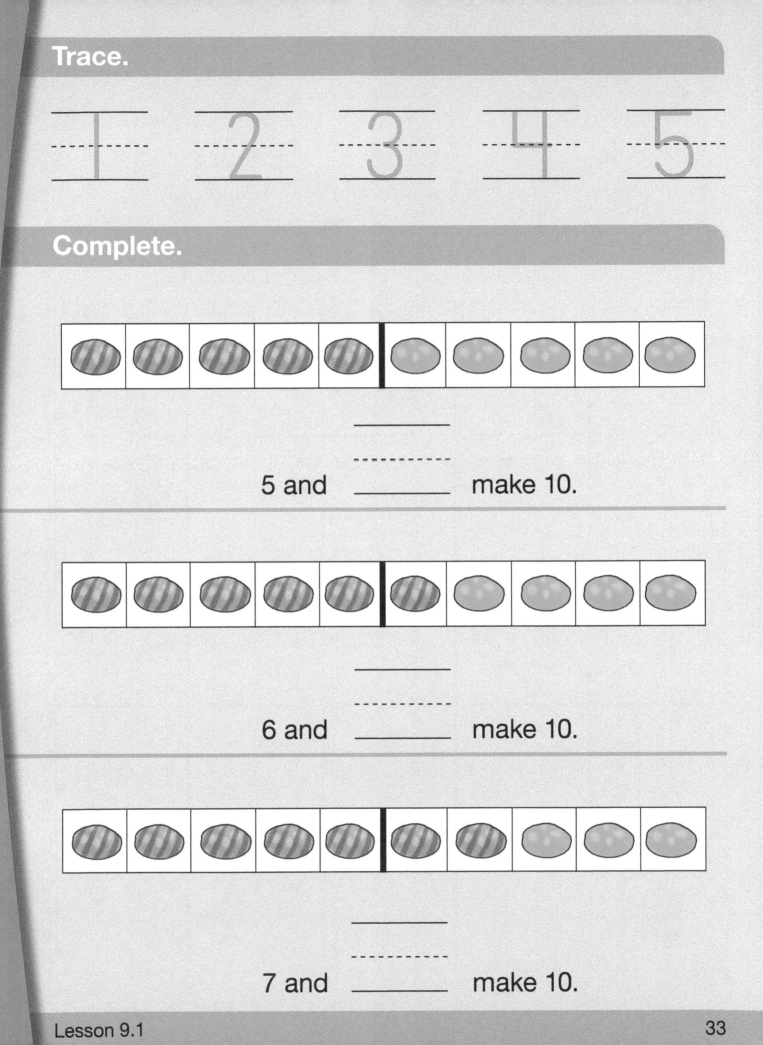

5 and _____ make 10.

6 and _____ make 10.

7 and _____ make 10.

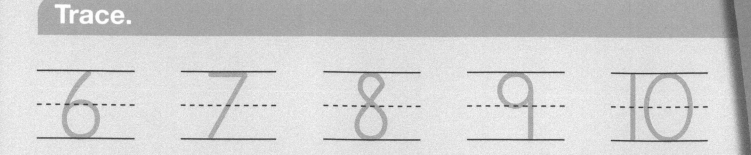

Trace.

6 7 8 9 10

Draw a path to the house. Watch out for the puddles.

Trace.

1 2 3 4 5

Match.

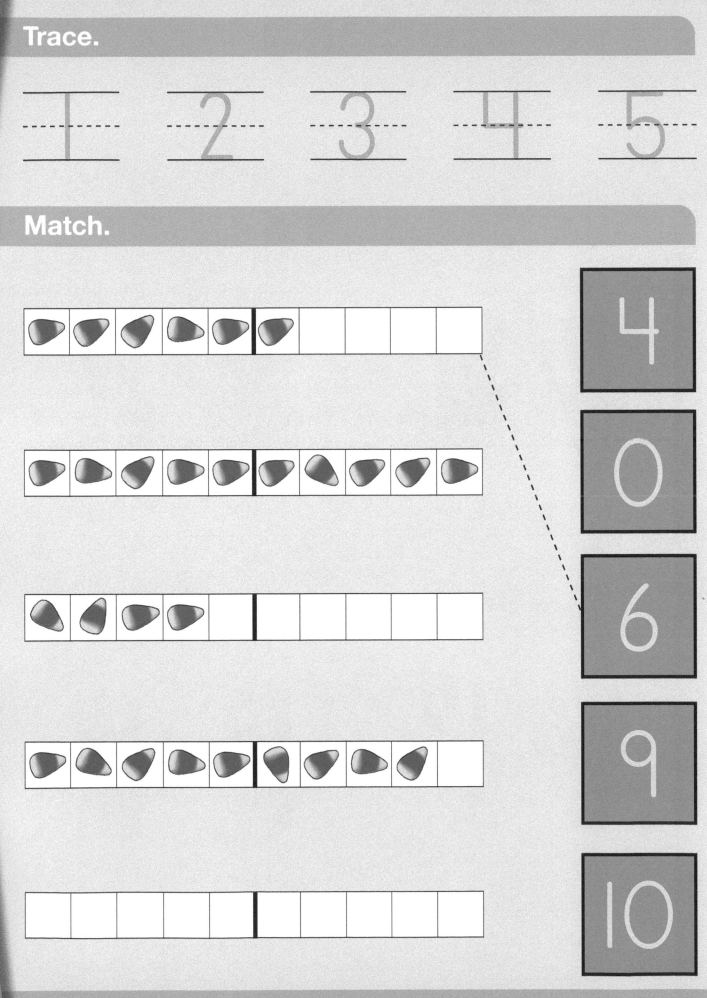

6   7   8   9   10

How many fingers are up?

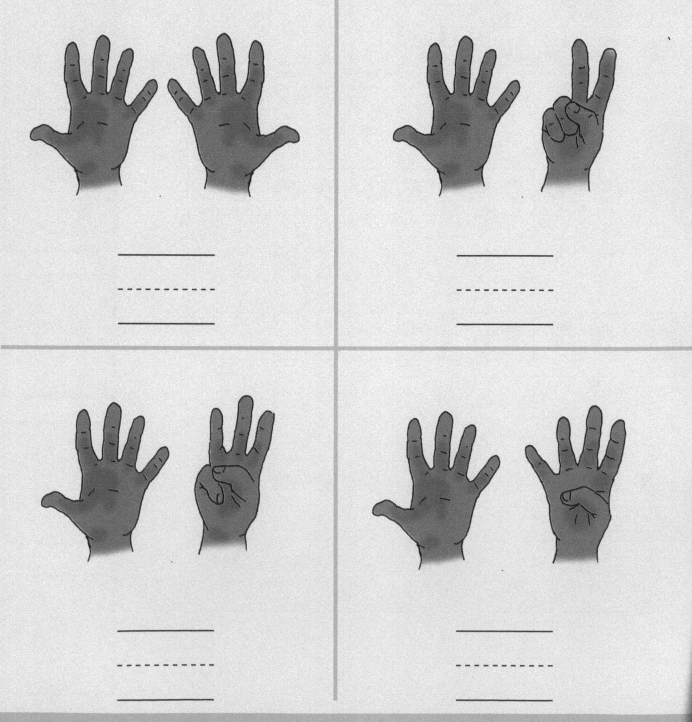

Trace.

5   4   3   2   1

Circle the fruit that comes next in the pattern.

Trace.

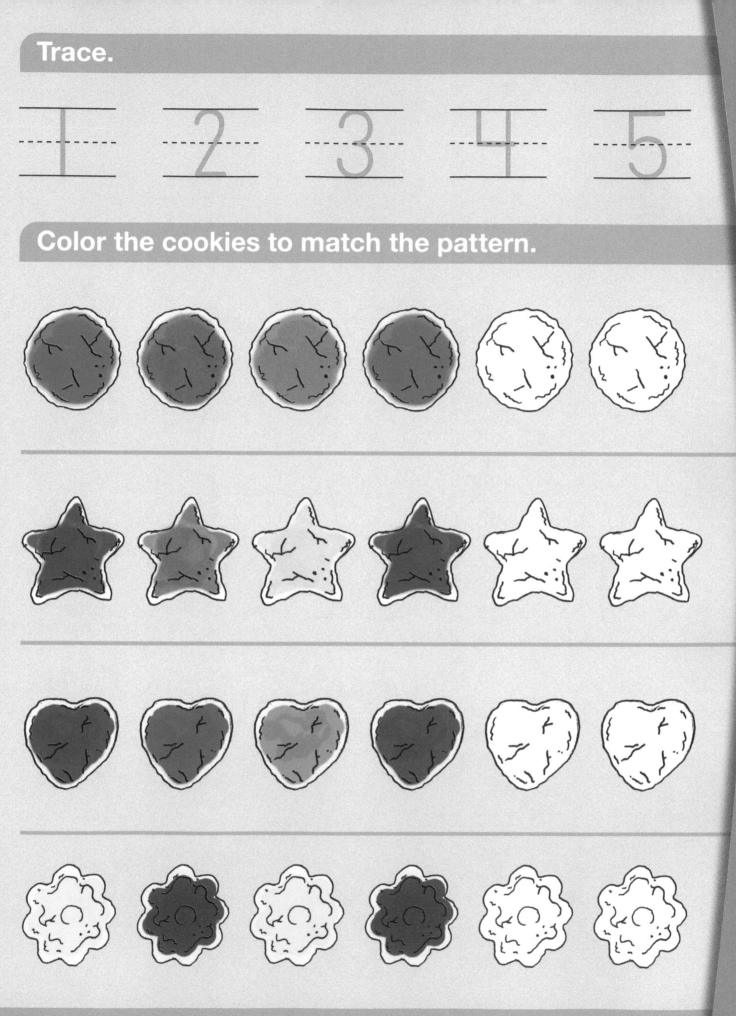

1   2   3   4   5

Color the cookies to match the pattern.

Trace.

6   7   8   9   10

Draw the next shape in the pattern.

6 7 8 9 10

Color the beads to complete the pattern.

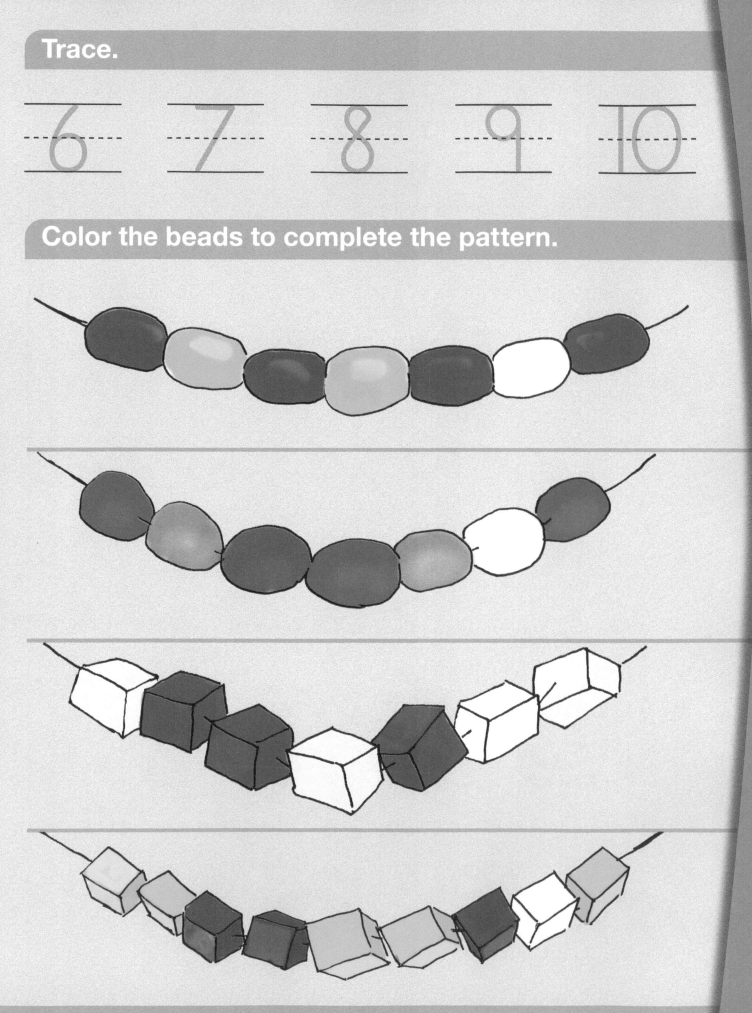

Trace.

10 9 8 7 6

Circle the taller tower.

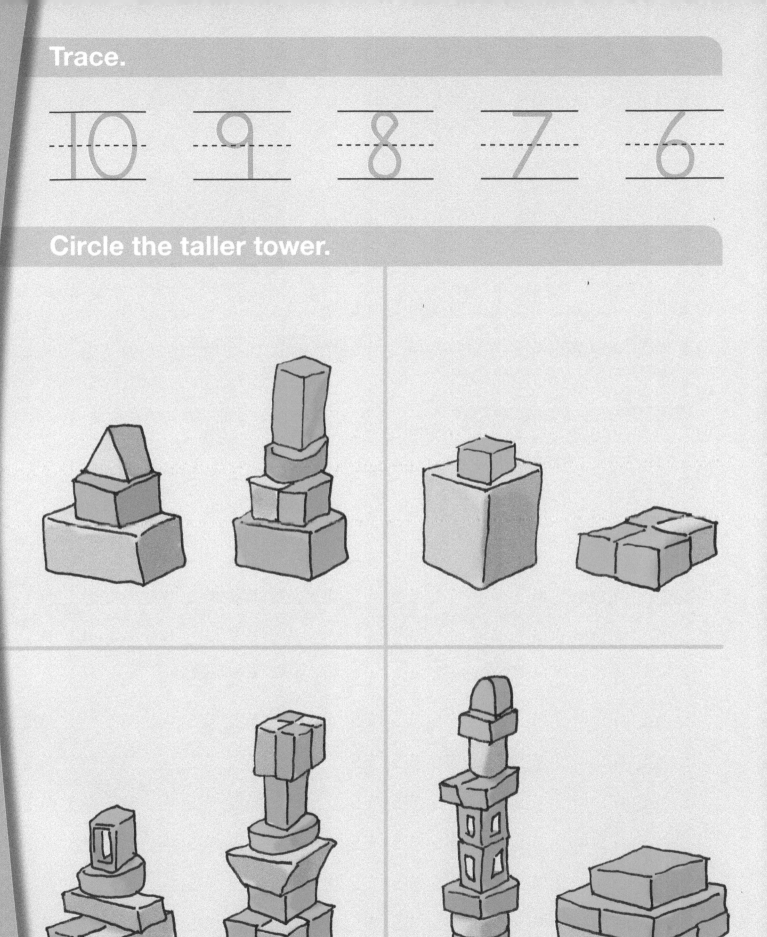

5 4 3 2 1

Circle the shorter line in each pair.

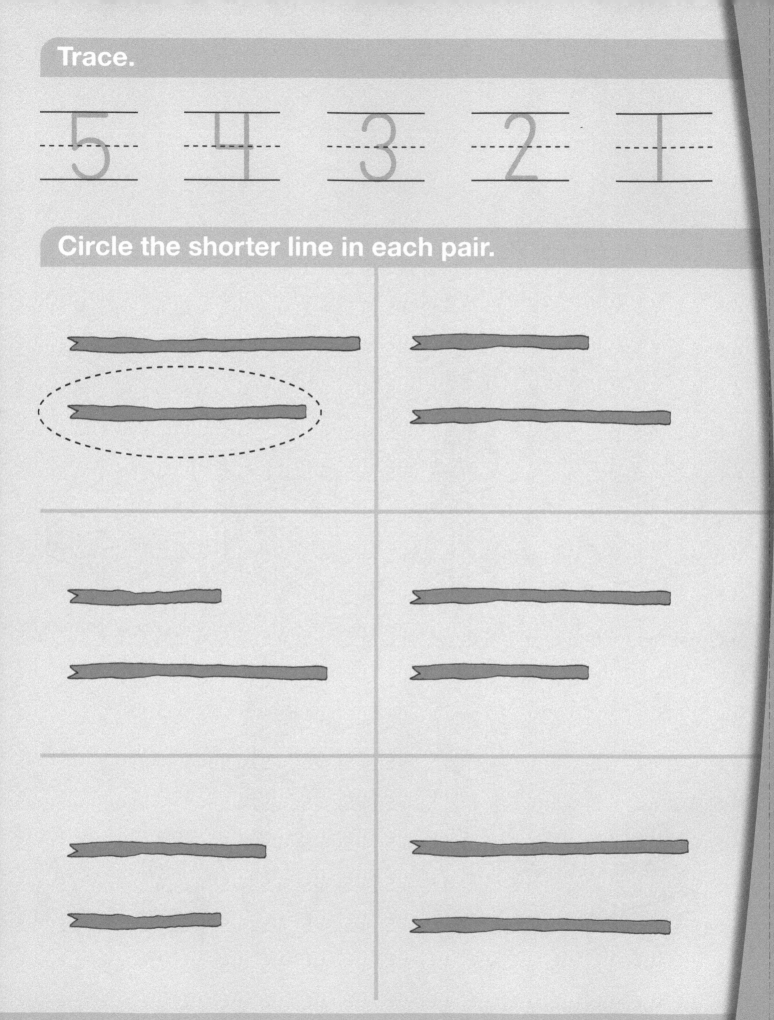

Trace.

10   9   8   7   6

Draw a longer pencil.

Draw a shorter ribbon.

Draw a straw that has an equal length.

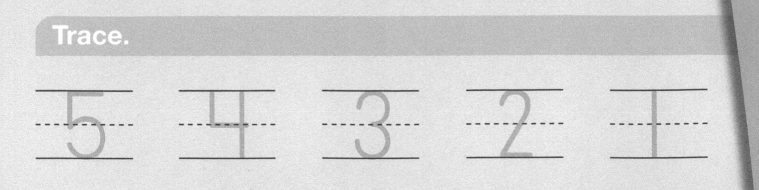

Trace.

5   4   3   2   1

Match the cups with equal amounts of water.

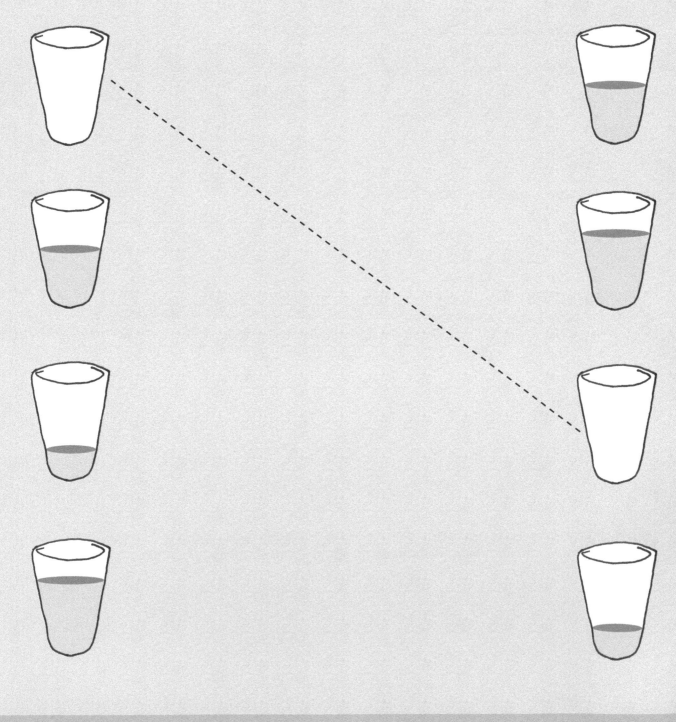

Trace.

Circle the group that has fewer.

Trace.

Draw an equal amount of tallies.

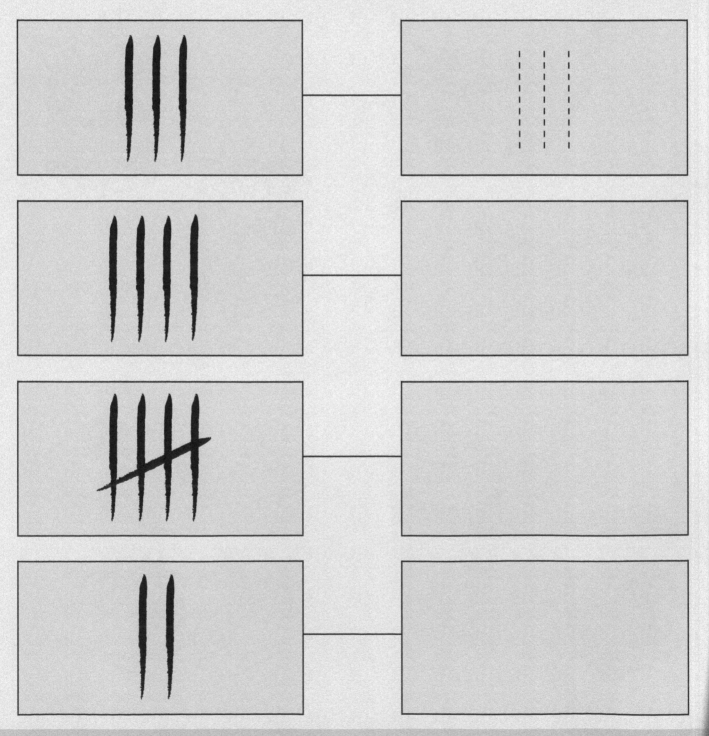

Trace.

1 2 3 4 5

Circle the ten-frame that has more.

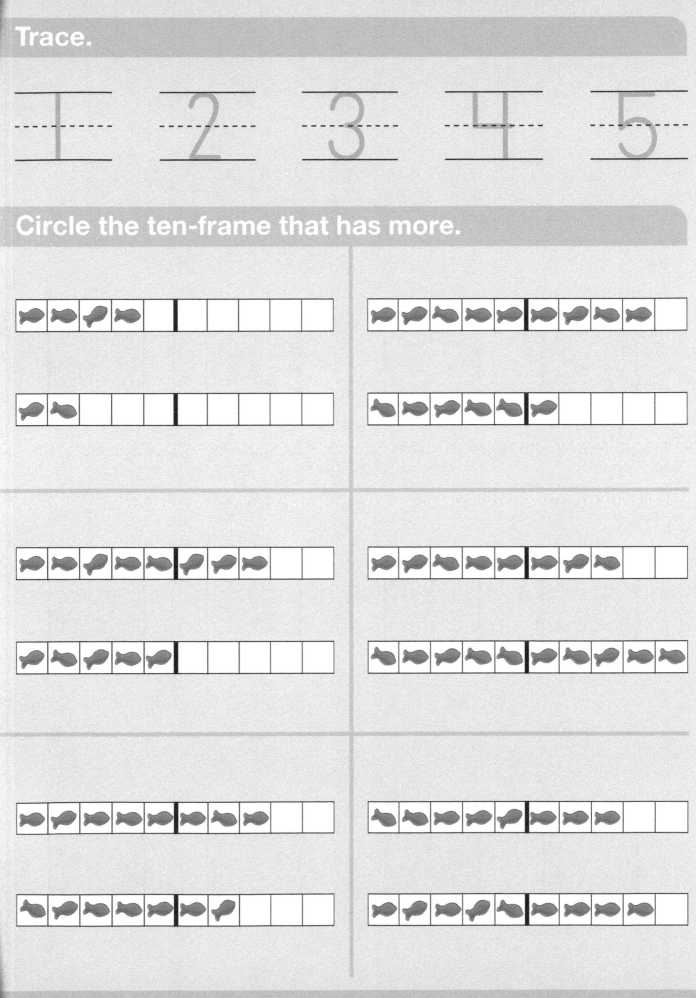

Trace.

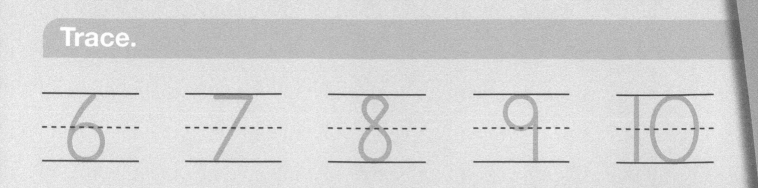

6 7 8 9 10

Circle the number that is greater.

4 8

5 0

3 7

8 6

10 9

8 9

Trace.

5   5   5   5   5

Circle the number that is greatest.
X the number that is least.

| 5 | 7 | 9 | | 3 | 1 | 4 |

| 10 | 6 | 2 | | 7 | 8 | 9 |

| 6 | 5 | 4 | | 3 | 9 | 6 |

8   5   9   10   3

The numbers are in order from least to greatest.
Write the numbers that are missing.

2 3 ____

6 7 ____

3 4 ____

7 8 ____

8 9 ____

1 2 ____

Trace.

1   3   7   4   6

The numbers are in order from least to greatest. Write the numbers that are missing.

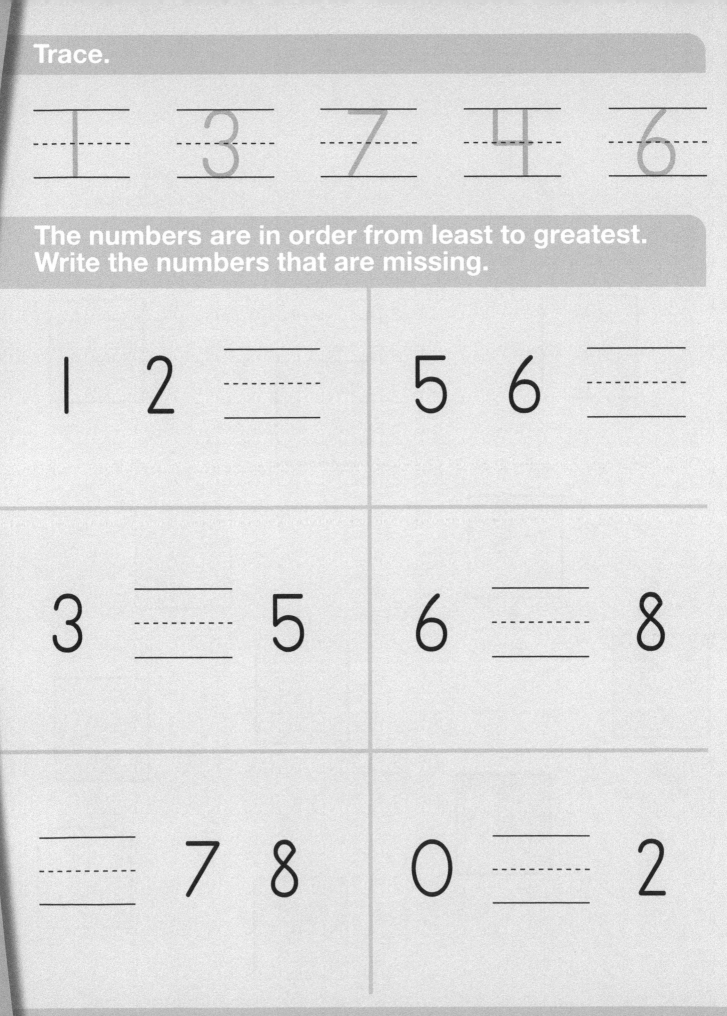

1   2   ___   5   6   ___

3   ___   5   6   ___   8

___   7   8   0   ___   2

Trace.

3 3 3 3 3

Connect the numbers in order from greatest to least.

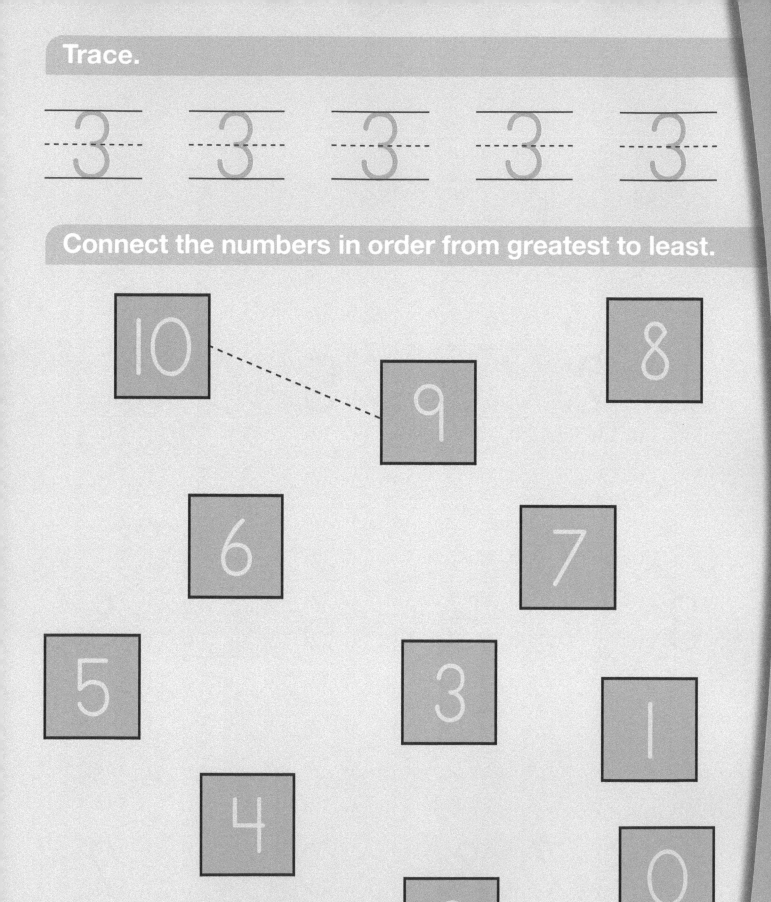

6   7   8   9   10

Complete.

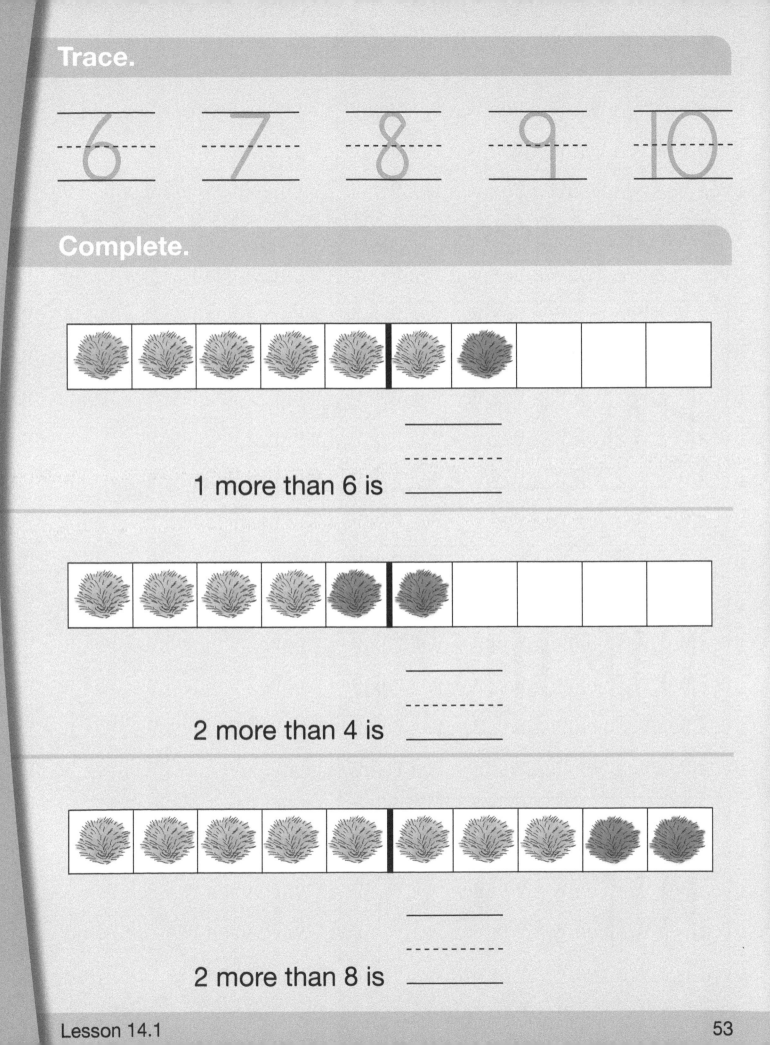

_____
- - - - - - - - -
1 more than 6 is _____

_____
- - - - - - - - -
2 more than 4 is _____

_____
- - - - - - - - -
2 more than 8 is _____

2   4   6   8   10

Draw 2 more tallies in each box. Complete the sentences.

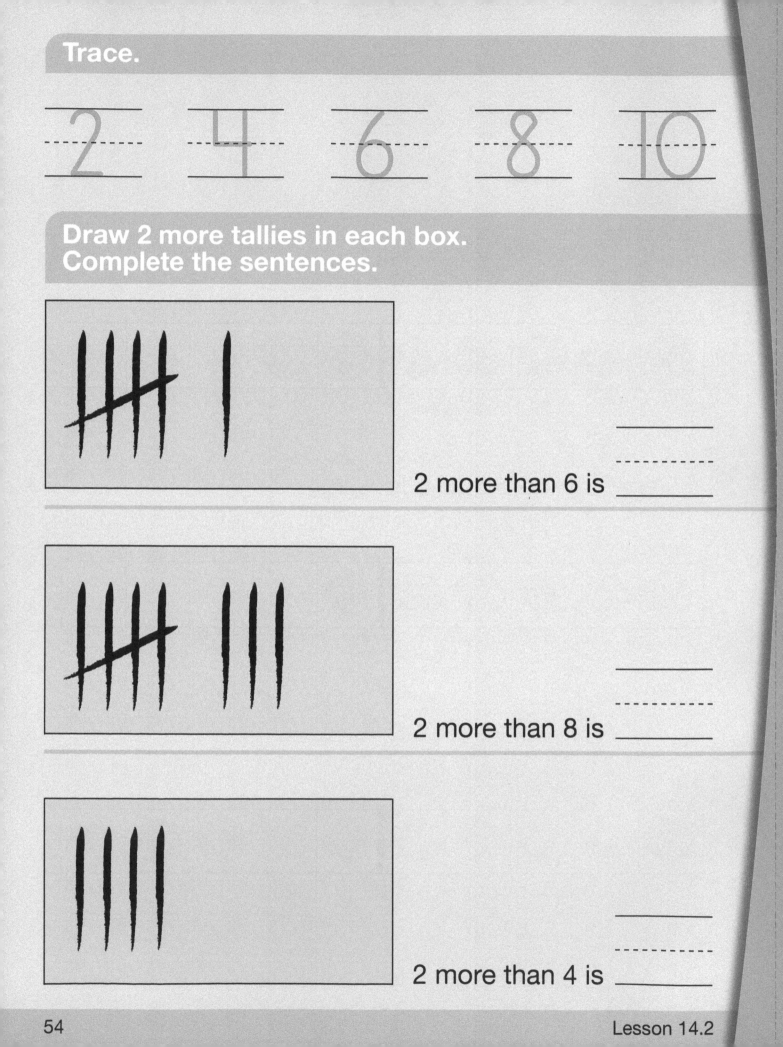

2 more than 6 is _____

2 more than 8 is _____

2 more than 4 is _____

1   3   5   7   9

Complete.

2 less than 5 is _____

2 less than 7 is _____

2 less than 9 is _____

2   4   6   8   10

Write how many.

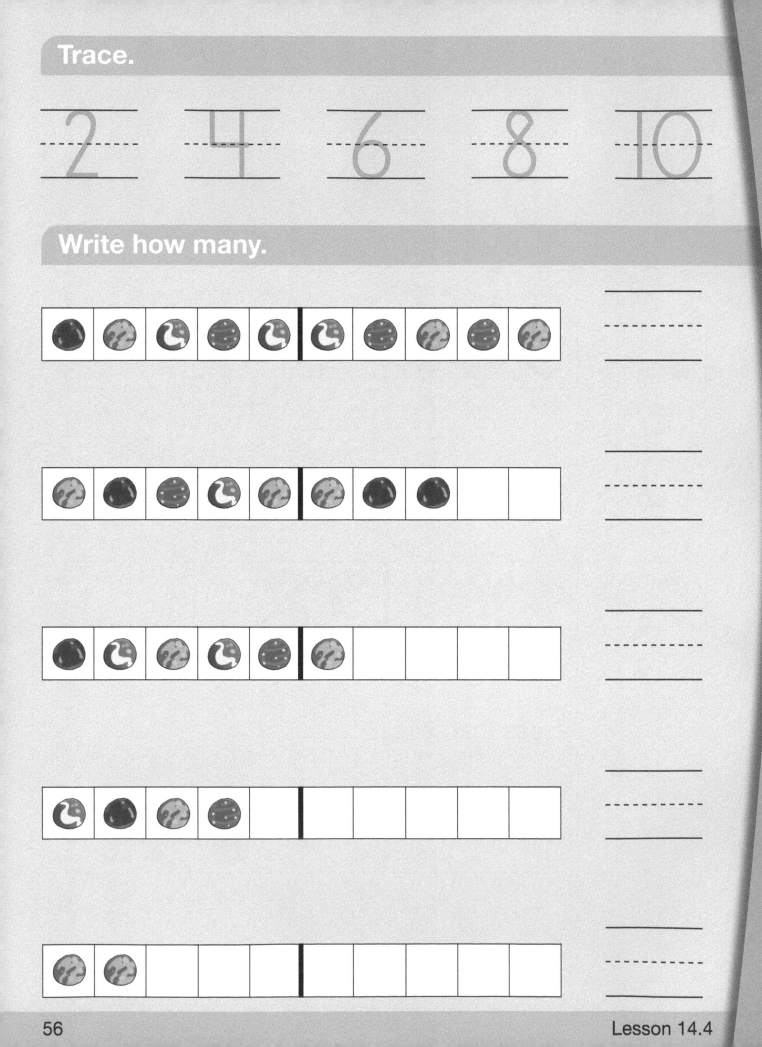

Trace.

Add 1 button.

Add 2 cookies.

Add 3 blocks.

Add 0 candles.

5   4   3   2   1

Write numbers to match.

2 + 4

___ + ___

___ + ___

___ + ___

Trace.

2   3   5   9   4

Write numbers to match.

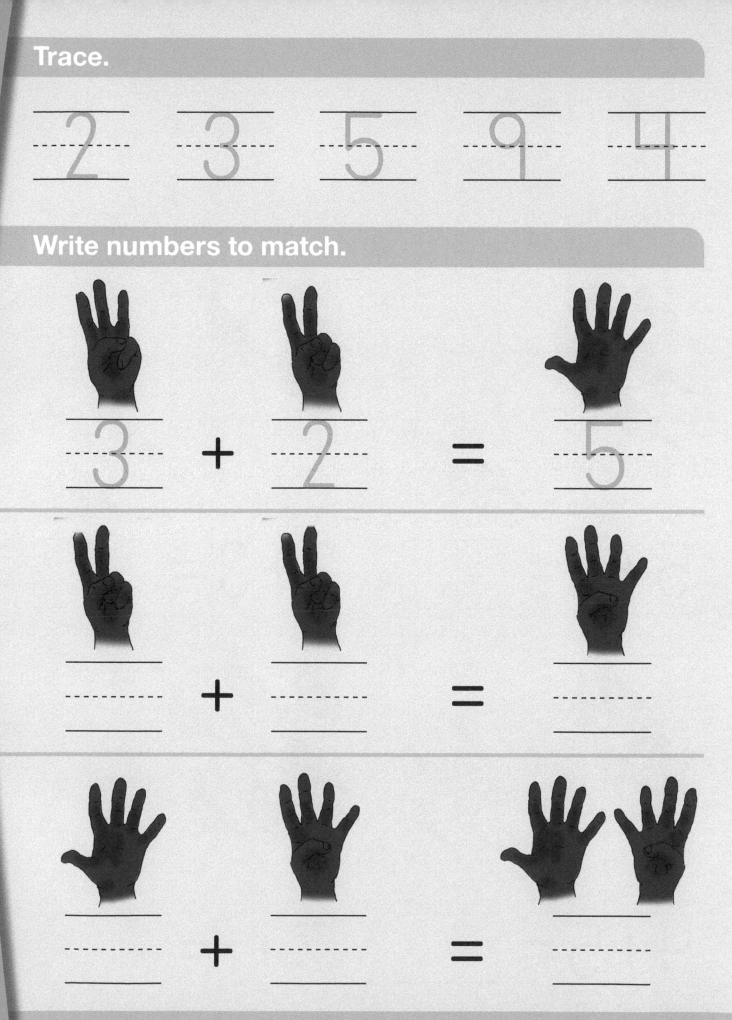

3 + 2 = 5

___ + ___ = ___

___ + ___ = ___

6   7   8   9   10

Solve.

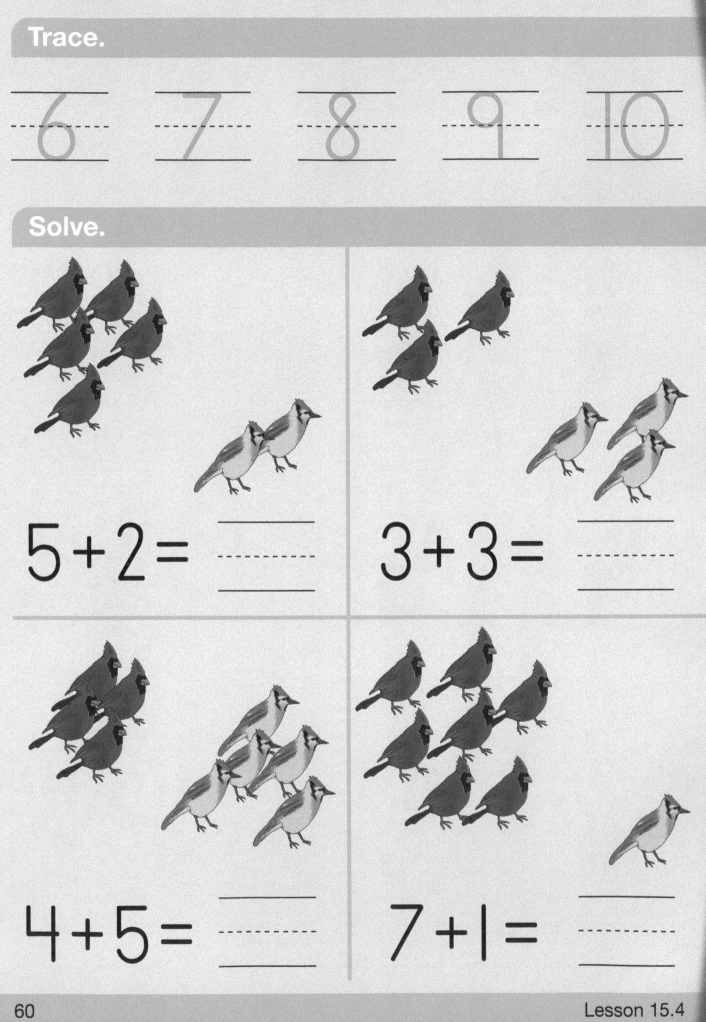

5 + 2 = _____

3 + 3 = _____

4 + 5 = _____

7 + 1 = _____

0   5   8   2   3

Draw a picture to match.

$$5 + 3 = 8$$

Trace.

6   3   1   4   7

Complete the equations to match the pictures.

3 + 4 = ____

5 + ____ = ____

____ + ____ = ____

____ + ____ = ____

Trace.

1 2 3 4 5

Complete the equations to match the pictures.

5 + 1 = ___

___ + ___ = ___

___ + ___ = ___

___ + ___ = ___

Trace.

5 6 7 8 9

Solve.

5 + 4 = _____

3 + 3 = _____

3 + 5 = _____

2 + 6 = _____

1 + 4 = _____

3 + 2 = _____

5 + 0 = _____

7 + 1 = _____

Trace.

7 9 3 8 4

Complete.

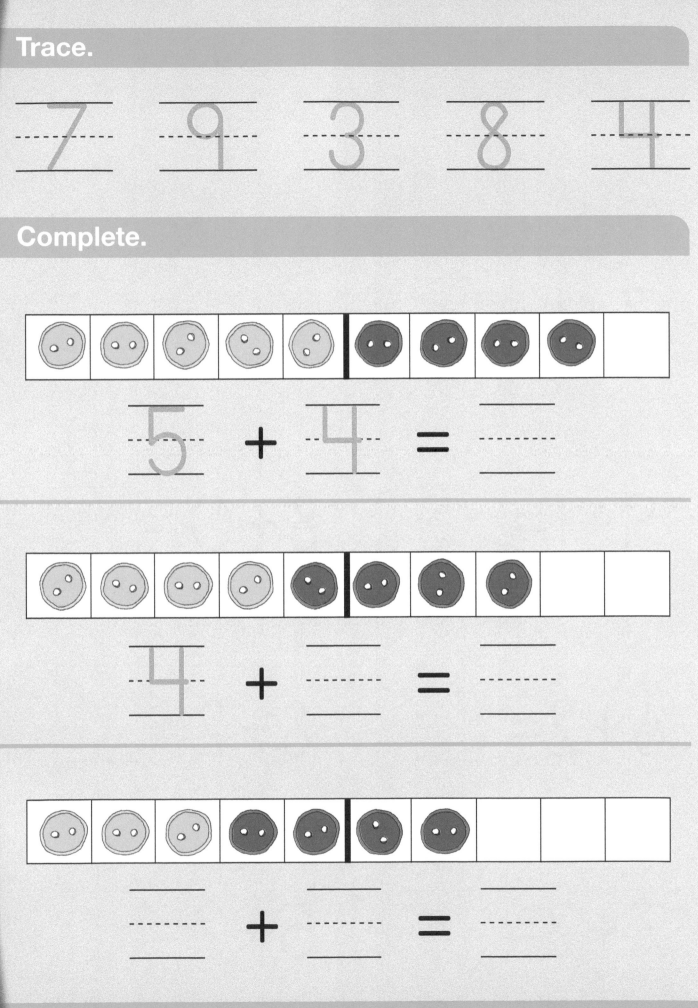

5 + 4 = ___

4 + ___ = ___

___ + ___ = ___

6   7   8   9   10

7 + 1 = _____   6 + 1 = _____

9 + 1 = _____   8 + 0 = _____

6 + 2 = _____   8 + 2 = _____

7 + 2 = _____   5 + 2 = _____

9   6   10   5   7

Solve.

5 + 3 = _____   5 + 0 = _____

5 + 4 = _____   5 + 2 = _____

5 + 5 = _____   5 + 1 = _____

0 + 5 = _____   1 + 5 = _____

Trace.

2 6 9 7 5

Solve.

$4 + 3 = \underline{\hspace{1cm}}$

$3 + 4 = \underline{\hspace{1cm}}$

$5 + 4 = \underline{\hspace{1cm}}$

$4 + 5 = \underline{\hspace{1cm}}$

$4 + 1 = \underline{\hspace{1cm}}$

$1 + 4 = \underline{\hspace{1cm}}$

$4 + 2 = \underline{\hspace{1cm}}$

$2 + 4 = \underline{\hspace{1cm}}$

7   9   3   8   4

Solve.

$2 + 2 =$ _____

$1 + 1 =$ _____

$2 + 3 =$ _____

$1 + 2 =$ _____

$4 + 4 =$ _____

$3 + 3 =$ _____

$4 + 5 =$ _____

$3 + 4 =$ _____

6   7   8   9   10

Solve.

5 + 5 = _____

5 + 4 = _____

8 + 2 = _____

8 + 1 = _____

6 + 4 = _____

6 + 3 = _____

7 + 3 = _____

7 + 2 = _____

Trace.

9 6 10 5 7

Write how many.

_____

- - - - - - -

_____

Trace.

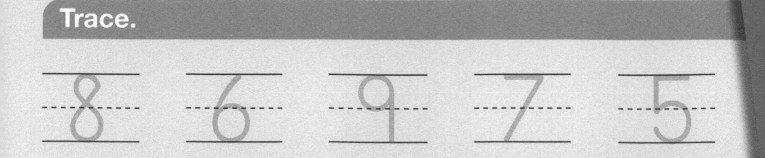

Draw fourteen circles.

Draw twenty Xs.

1   2   3   4   5

Complete.

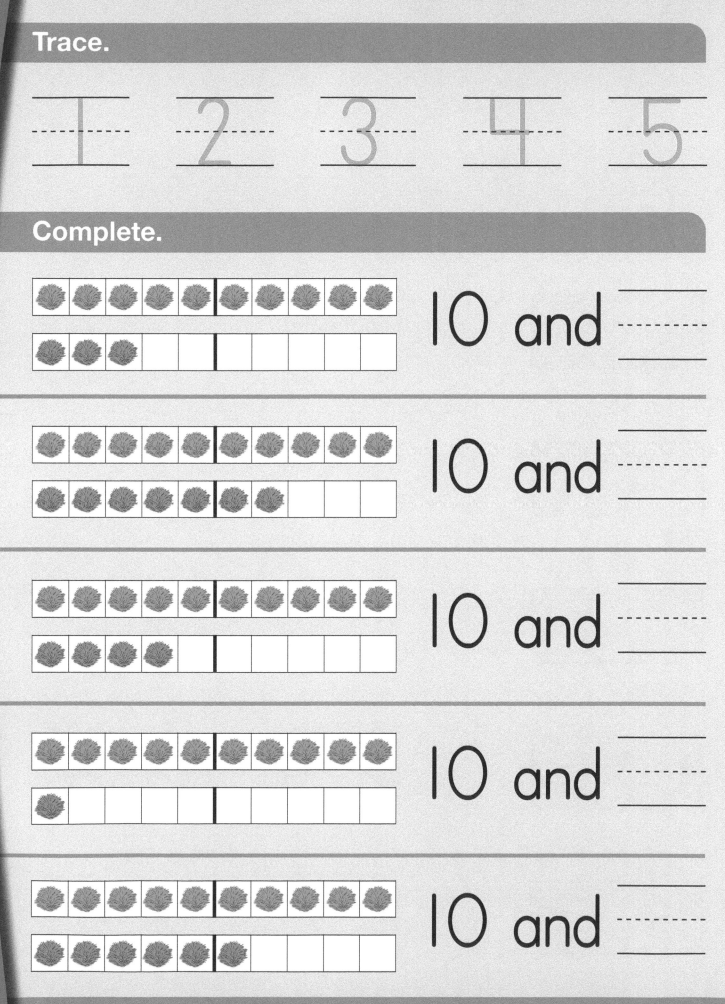

10 and ____

10 and ____

10 and ____

10 and ____

10 and ____

Trace.

6   7   8   9   10

Match.

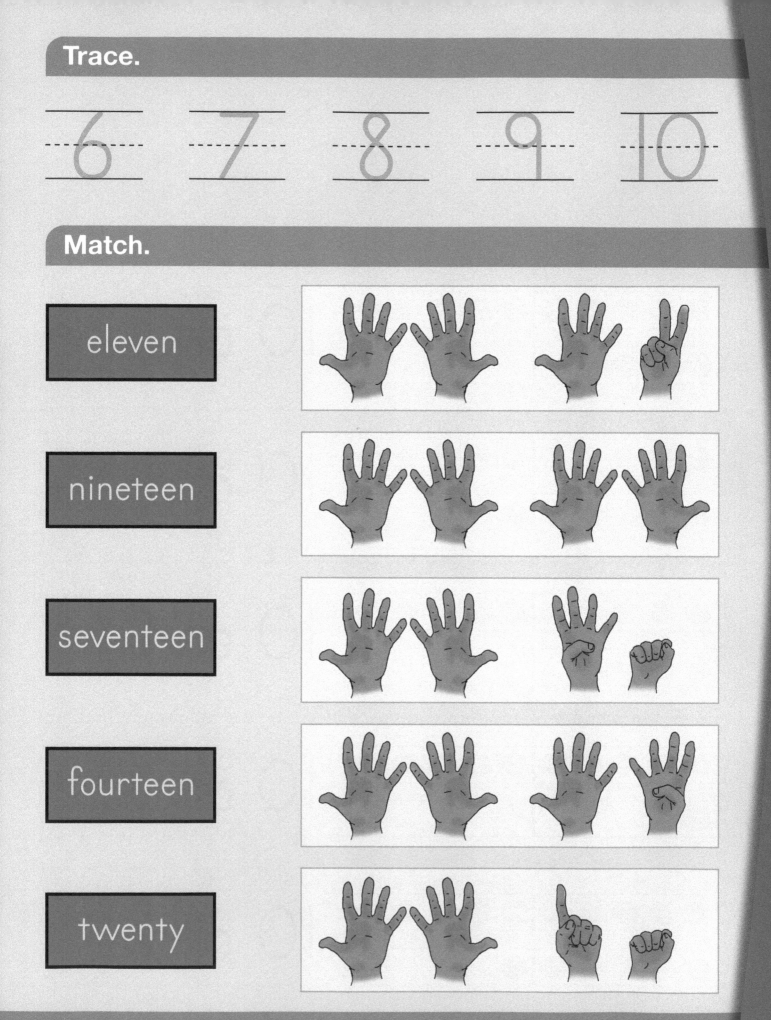

eleven

nineteen

seventeen

fourteen

twenty

10 9 8 7 6

Match.

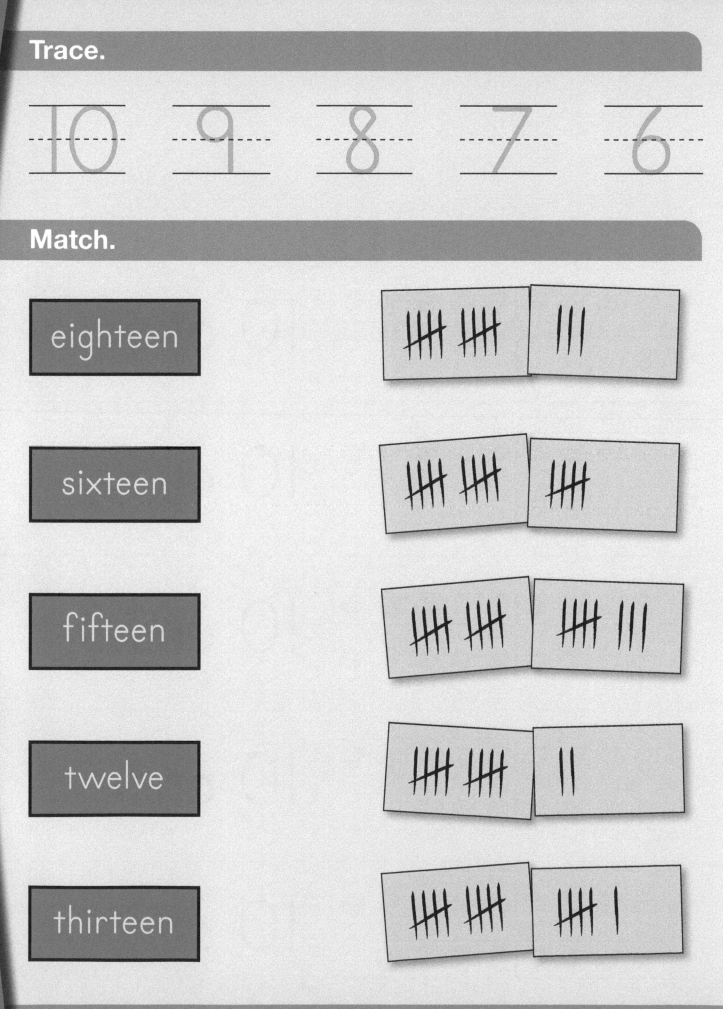

eighteen

sixteen

fifteen

twelve

thirteen

5 4 3 2 1

Complete.

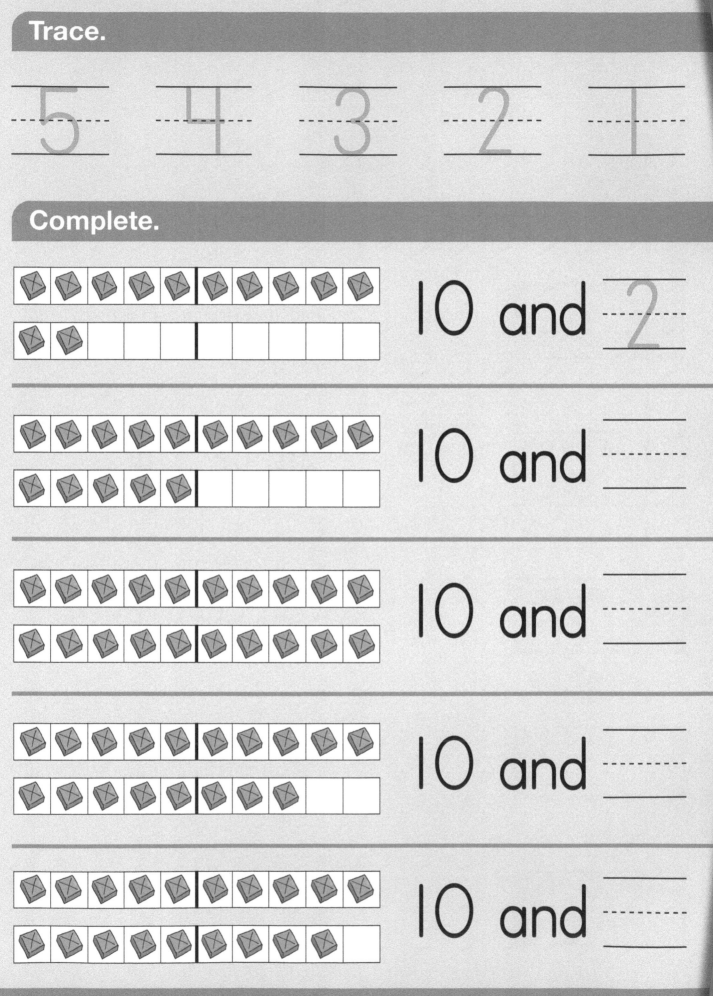

10 and 2

10 and ___

10 and ___

10 and ___

10 and ___

Trace.

Match.

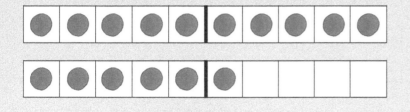

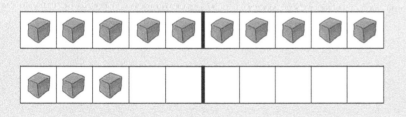

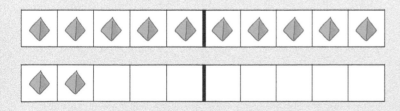

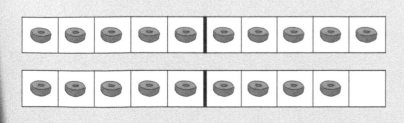

Color circles to match.

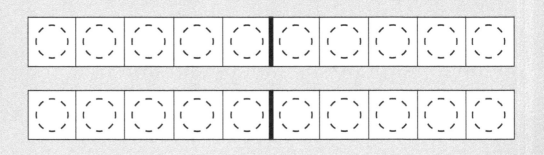

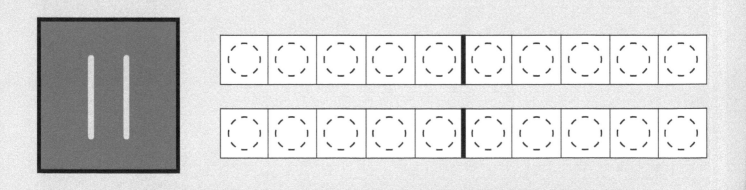

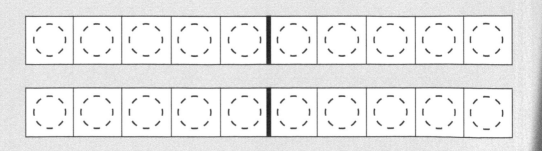

Trace.

Connect the dots in order.

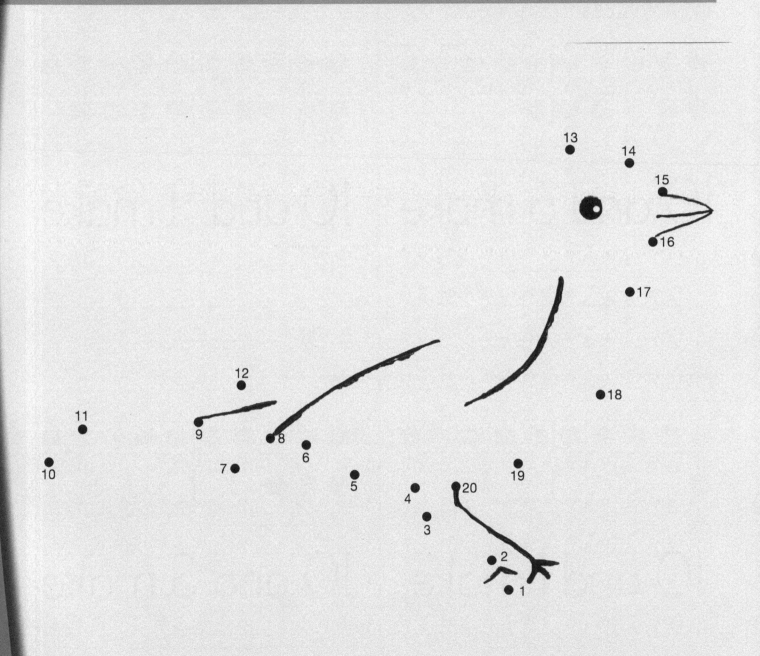

5   4   3   2   1

Complete.

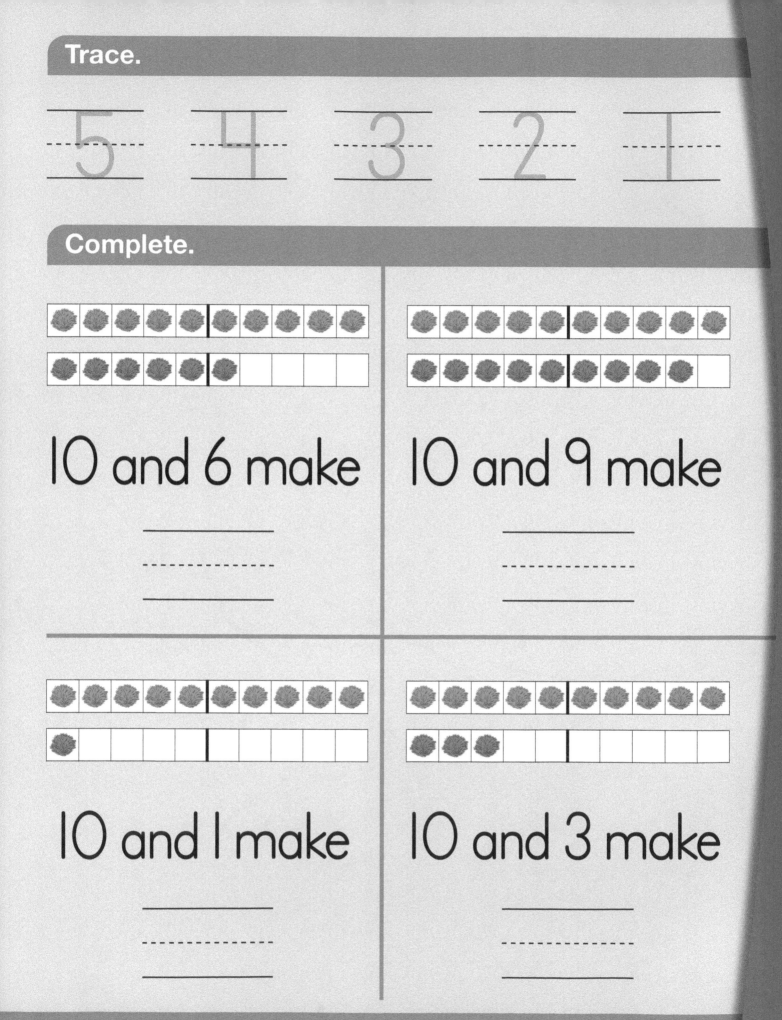

10 and 6 make

_____

- - - - - - - -

_____

10 and 9 make

_____

- - - - - - - -

_____

10 and 1 make

_____

- - - - - - - -

_____

10 and 3 make

_____

- - - - - - - -

_____

Trace.

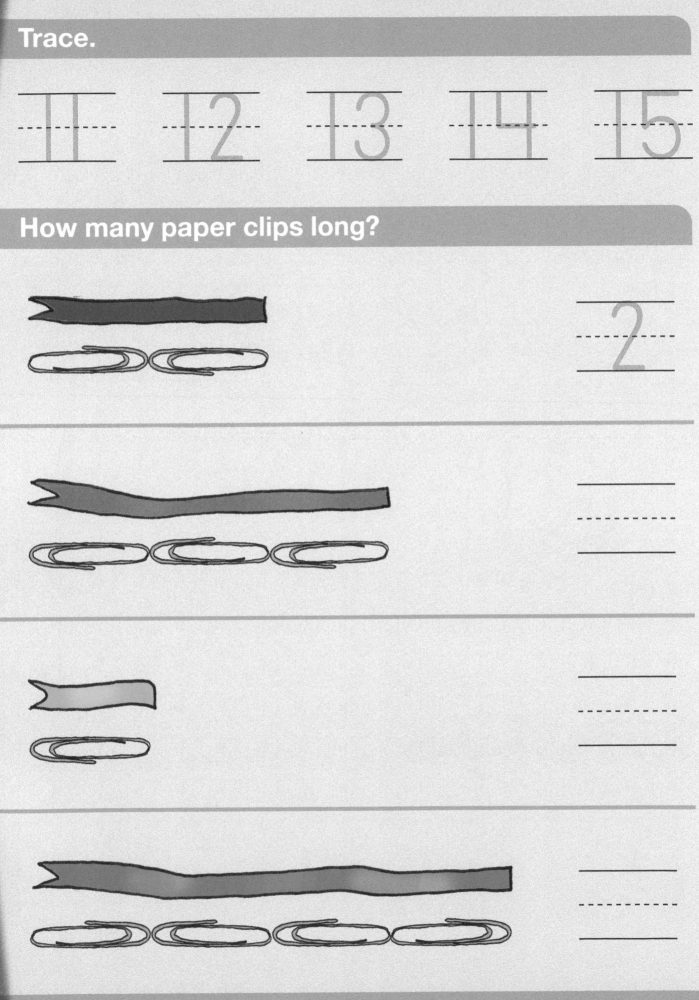

How many paper clips long?

2

Trace.

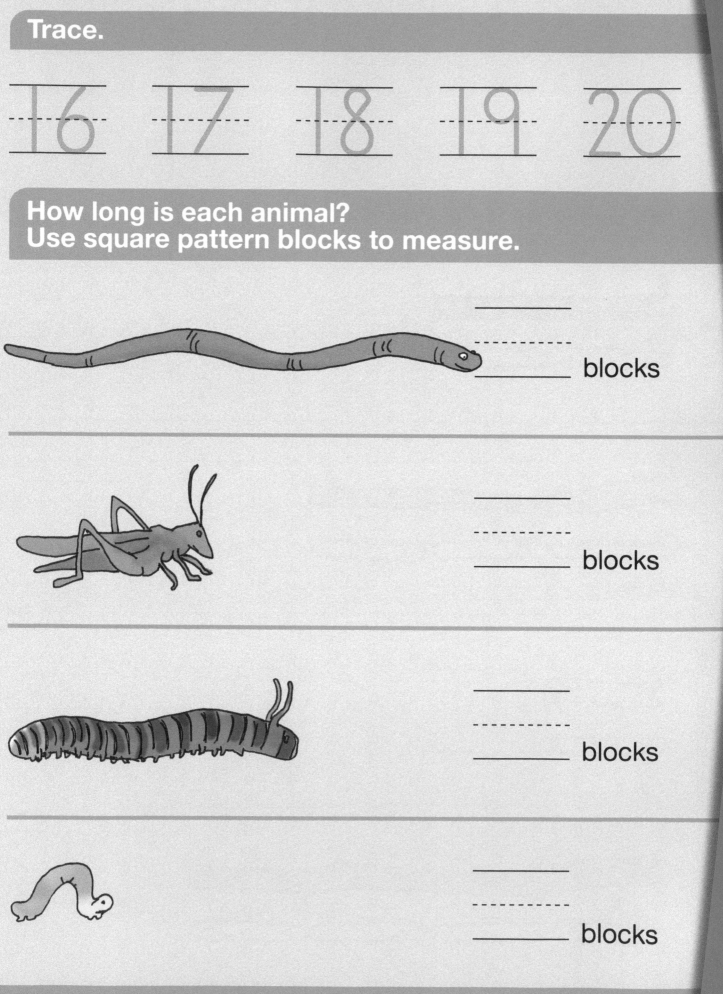

16 17 18 19 20

How long is each animal?
Use square pattern blocks to measure.

_____ blocks

_____ blocks

_____ blocks

_____ blocks

Lesson 21.2

Trace.

11 12 13 14 15

How long is each stick?
Use square pattern blocks to measure.

_____

_____ blocks

_____

_____ blocks

_____

_____ blocks

_____

_____ blocks

16 17 18 19 20

How tall is each paper cut-out?
Use square pattern blocks to measure.

_____ blocks   _____ blocks   _____ blocks

Trace.

11 12 13 14 15

Circle the heavier animal in each pair.
X the lighter animal in each pair.

Trace.

Draw something that's heavy.

Draw something that's light.

Lesson 22.2

Trace.

Circle the container that holds more in each pair.
X the container that holds less in each pair.

Trace.

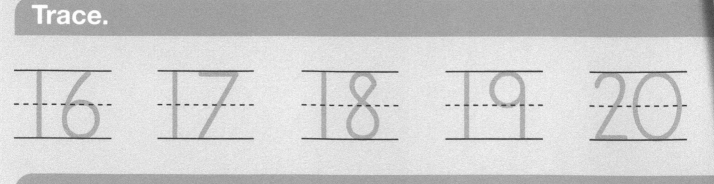

Circle the container that holds the most in each set.
X the container that holds the least in each set.

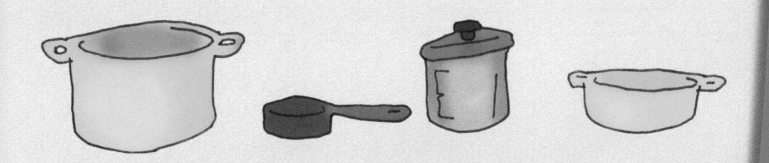

Lesson 22.4

Trace.

Cross out 2.

How many are left? _____

Cross out 1.

How many are left? _____

Cross out 4.

How many are left? _____

Cross out 3.

How many are left? _____

2 2 2 2 2

Solve.

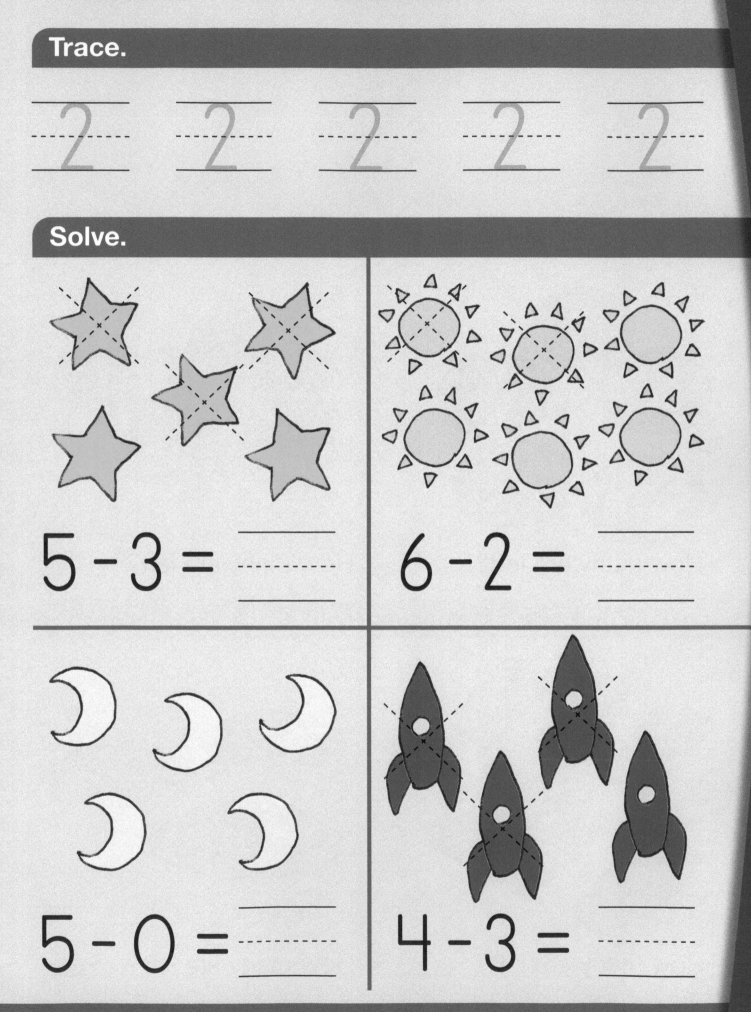

5 - 3 = _____

6 - 2 = _____

5 - 0 = _____

4 - 3 = _____

3   3   3   3   3

X the balloons to match the equation and solve.

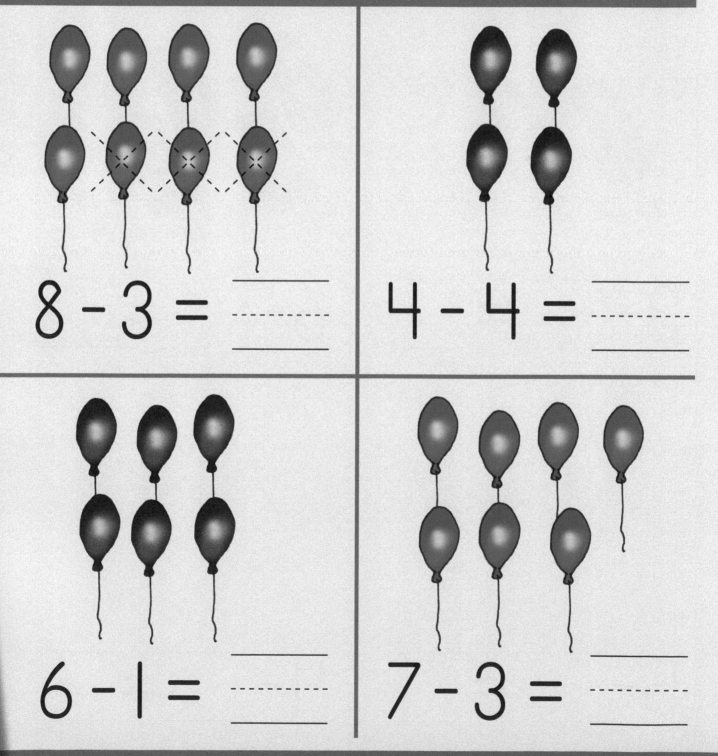

8 - 3 = _____

4 - 4 = _____

6 - 1 = _____

7 - 3 = _____

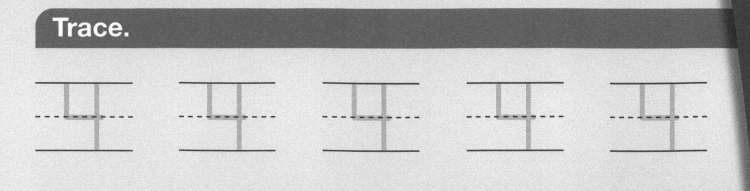

Complete and solve.

$3 - \text{\_\_\_} = \text{\_\_\_}$

$6 - \text{\_\_\_} = \text{\_\_\_}$

$5 - \text{\_\_\_} = \text{\_\_\_}$

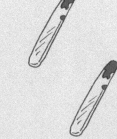

$4 - \text{\_\_\_} = \text{\_\_\_}$

Lesson 23.4

5   5   5   5   5

Solve.

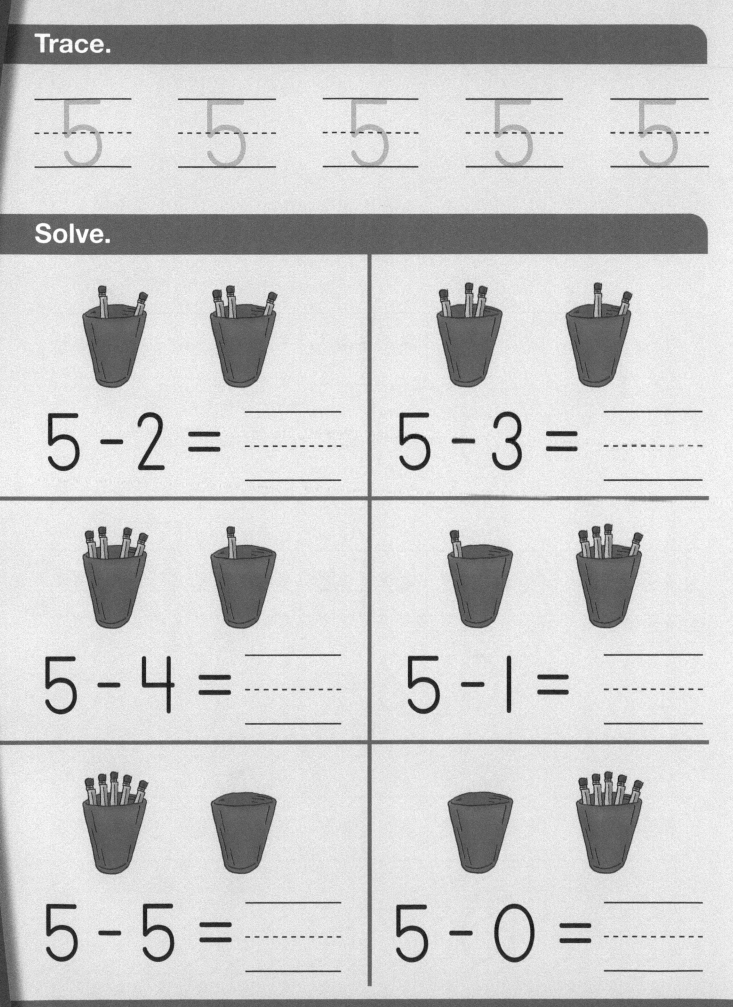

5 - 2 = _____

5 - 3 = _____

5 - 4 = _____

5 - 1 = _____

5 - 5 = _____

5 - 0 = _____

6   6   6   6   6

Solve.

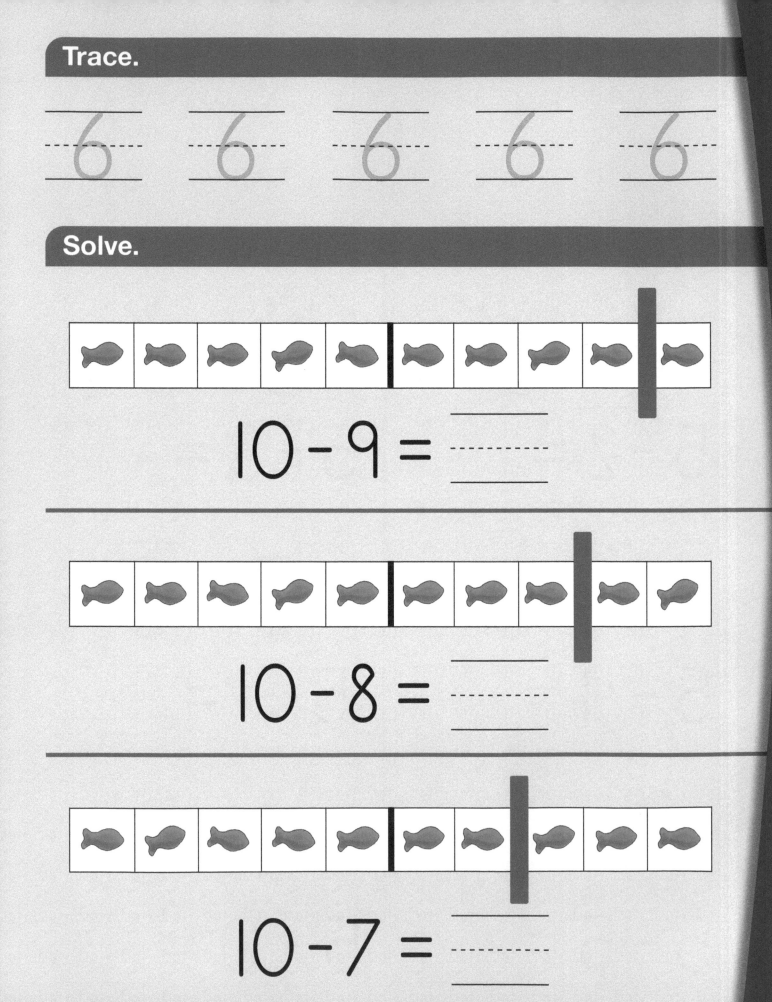

$$10 - 9 = \underline{\hspace{2cm}}$$

$$10 - 8 = \underline{\hspace{2cm}}$$

$$10 - 7 = \underline{\hspace{2cm}}$$

Trace.

7   7   7   7   7

Solve.

8 - 7 = _____

8 - 5 = _____

8 - 4 = _____

8 - 6 = _____

8   8   8   8   8

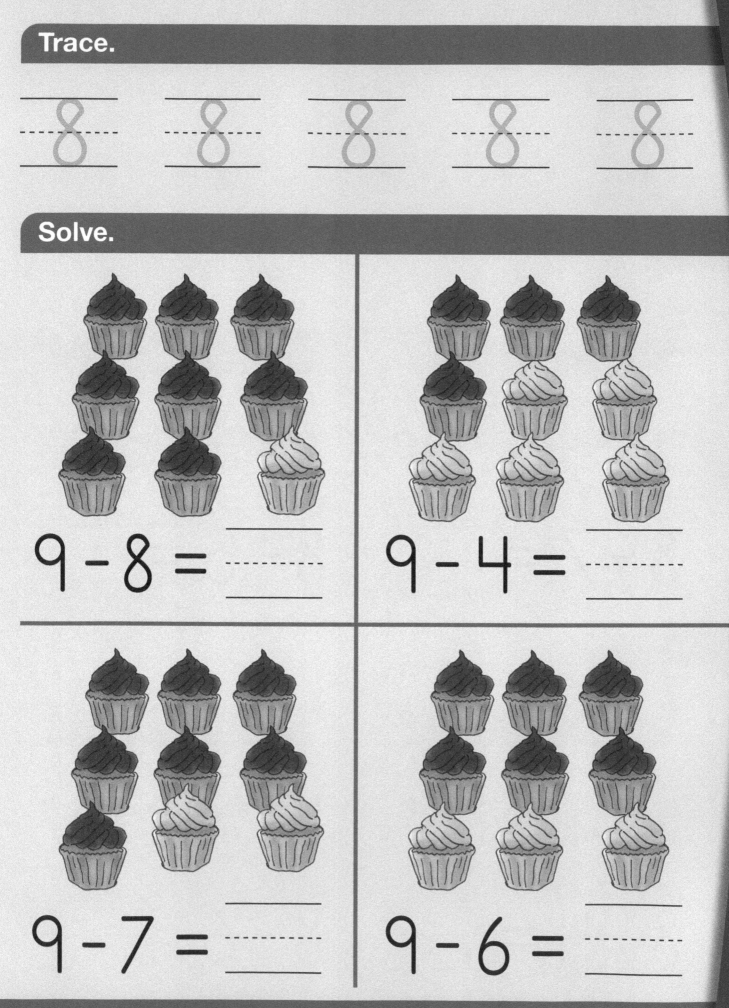

9 − 8 = _____

9 − 4 = _____

9 − 7 = _____

9 − 6 = _____

Trace.

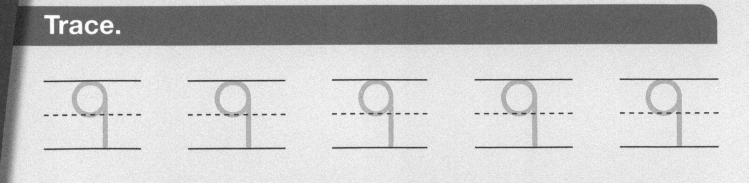

Solve.

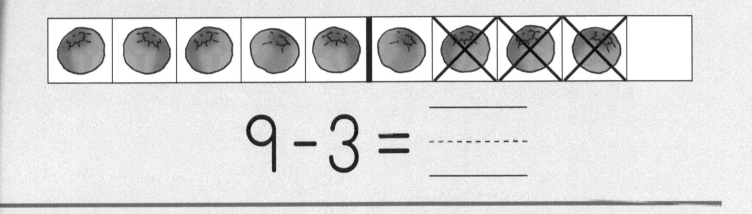

$$9 - 3 = \underline{\quad}$$

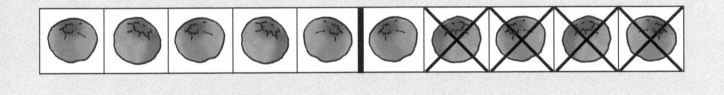

$$10 - 4 = \underline{\quad}$$

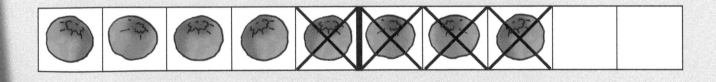

$$8 - 4 = \underline{\quad}$$

Trace.

10 10 10 10 10

Solve.

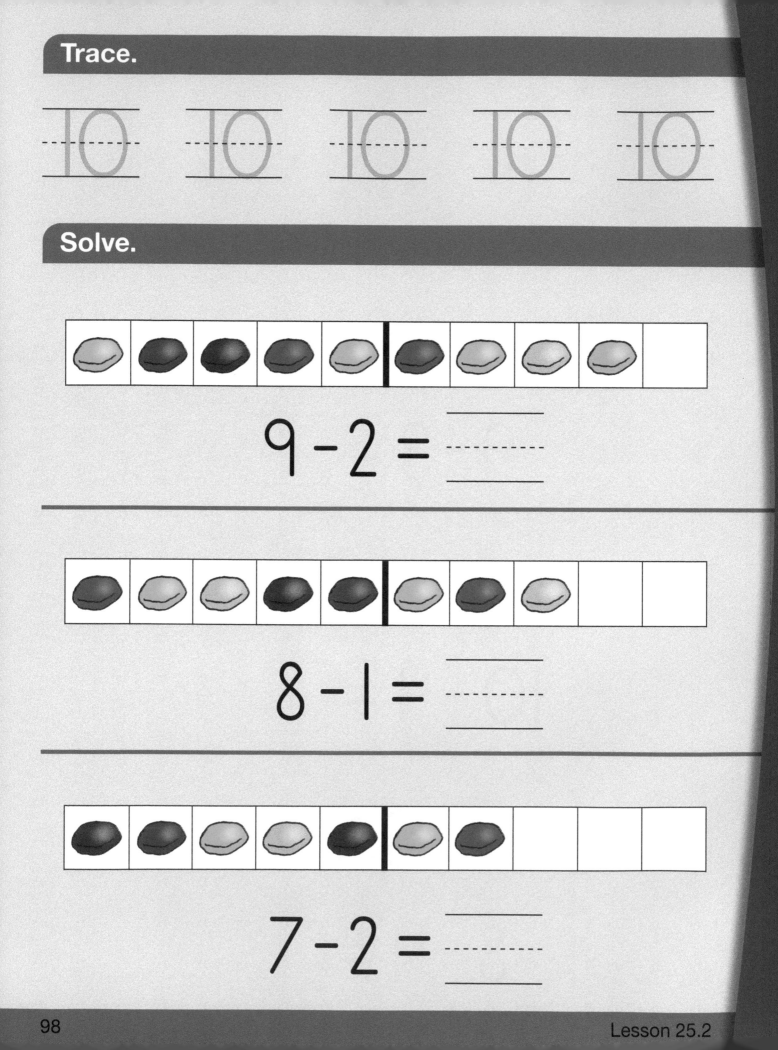

$9 - 2 =$ _____

$8 - 1 =$ _____

$7 - 2 =$ _____

Trace.

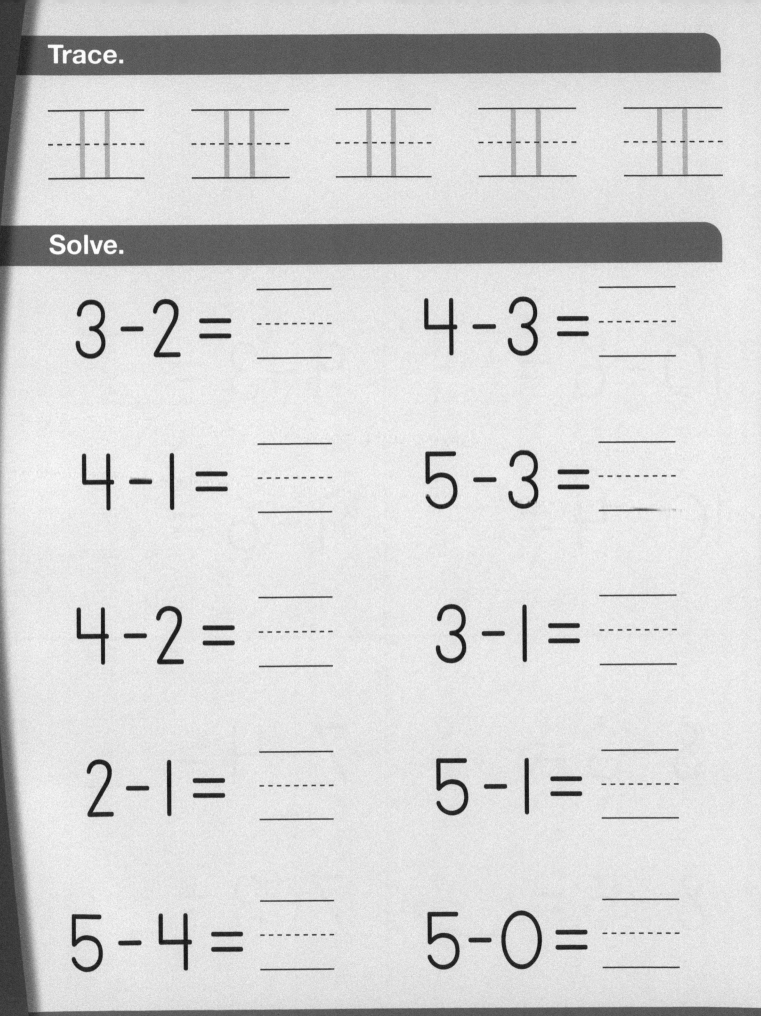

Solve.

3 - 2 = _____   4 - 3 = _____

4 - 1 = _____   5 - 3 = _____

4 - 2 = _____   3 - 1 = _____

2 - 1 = _____   5 - 1 = _____

5 - 4 = _____   5 - 0 = _____

12   12   12   12   12

Solve.

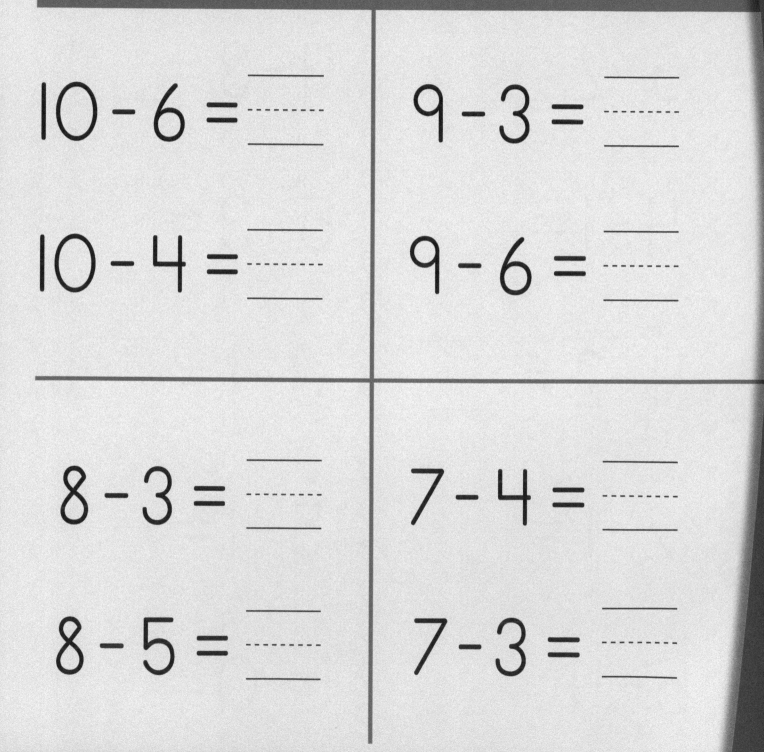

$10 - 6 =$ _____

$10 - 4 =$ _____

$9 - 3 =$ _____

$9 - 6 =$ _____

$8 - 3 =$ _____

$8 - 5 =$ _____

$7 - 4 =$ _____

$7 - 3 =$ _____

13   13   13   13   13

Write how many.

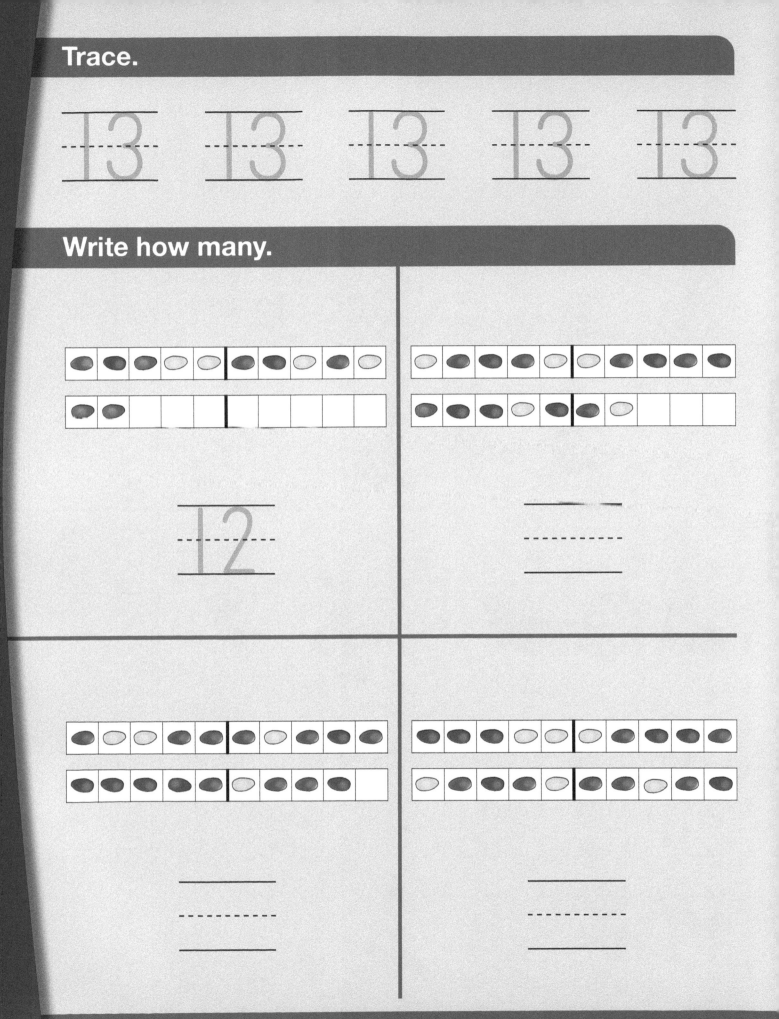

12

Trace.

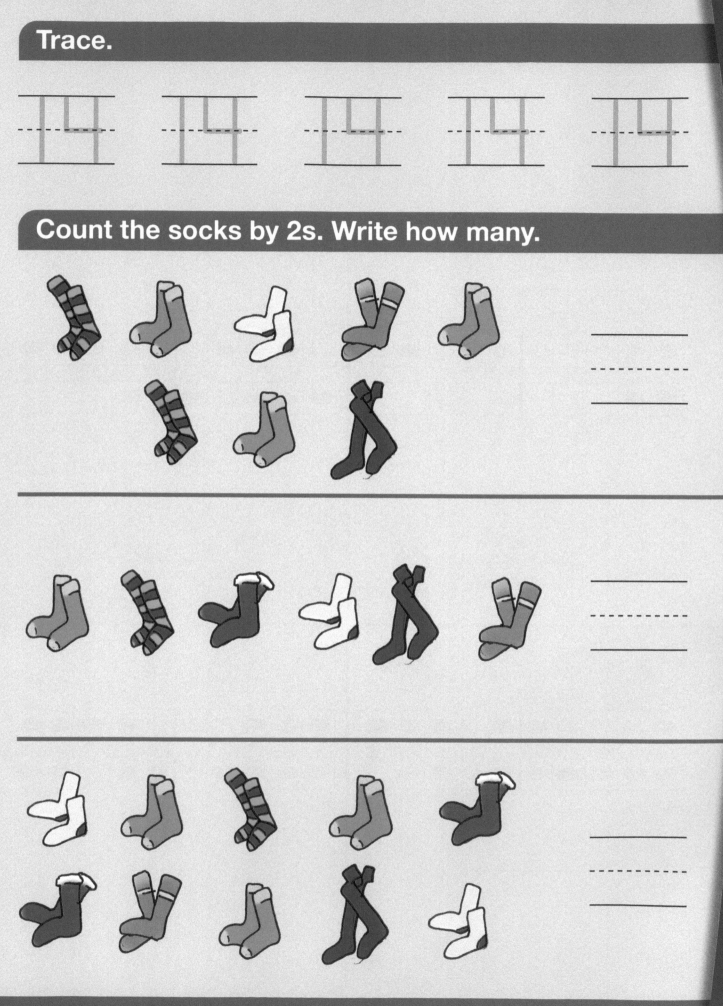

Count the socks by 2s. Write how many.

_____

_ _ _ _ _ _

_____

_____

_ _ _ _ _ _

_____

_____

_ _ _ _ _ _

_____

Lesson 26.2

Trace.

Match.

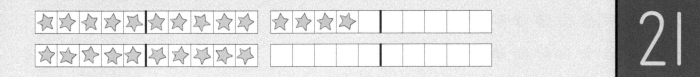

21

24

30

27

Trace.

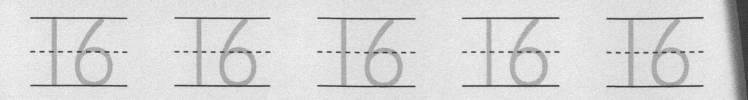

Match.

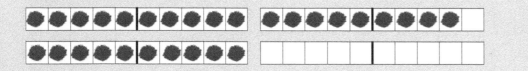

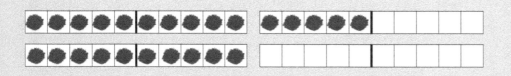

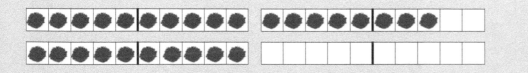

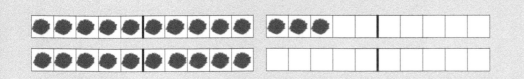

Trace.

17   17   17   17   17   17

Count the mittens by 2s. Write how many.

Trace.

Match. Each bag has 10 marbles.

Lesson 27.2

Trace.

Write how many. Each bag has 10 cookies.

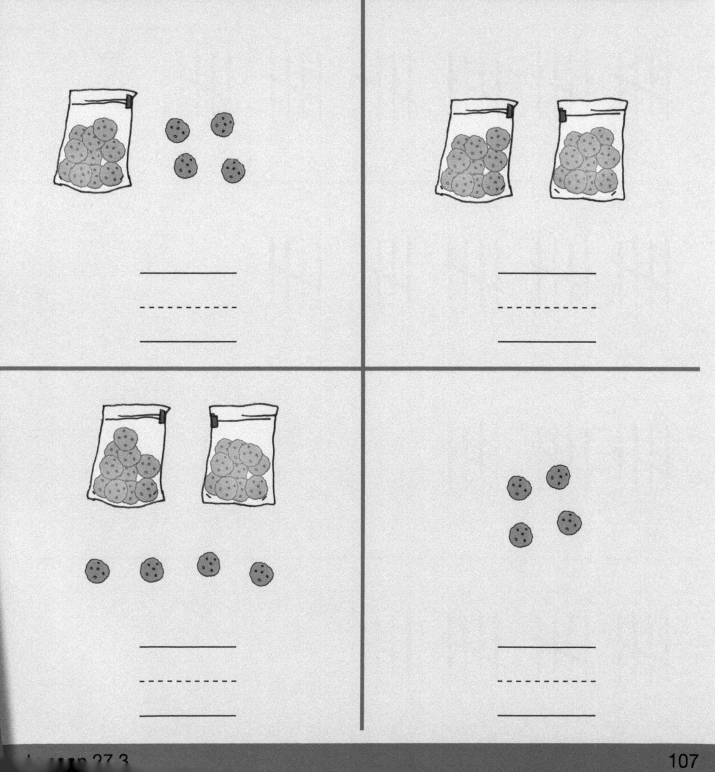

20   20   20   20   20

Count by 5s. Write how many.

卌 卌 卌 卌 卌 卌 _____

卌 卌 卌 卌 卌 _____

卌 卌 卌 _____

卌 卌 卌 卌 _____

Trace.

1   2   3   4   5

Match. Each bag has 10 cookies.

10

20

30

40

50

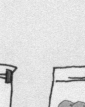

6   7   8   9   10

Count by 10s. Write how many.

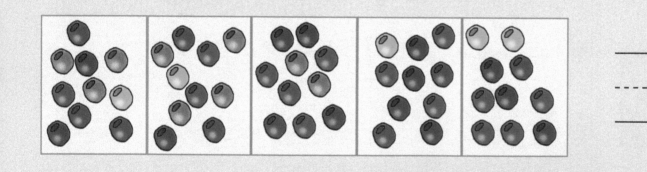

_____
- - - - - - - - - -
_____

_____
- - - - - - - - - -
_____

_____
- - - - - - - - - -
_____

Trace.

Connect the dots in order.

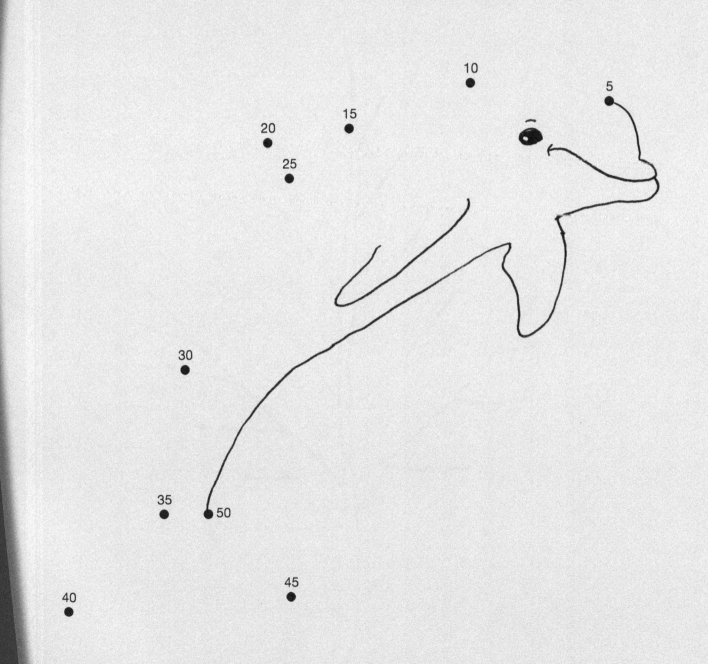

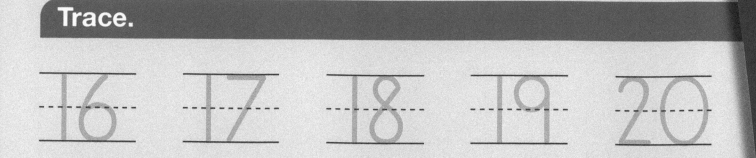

Connect the dots in order.

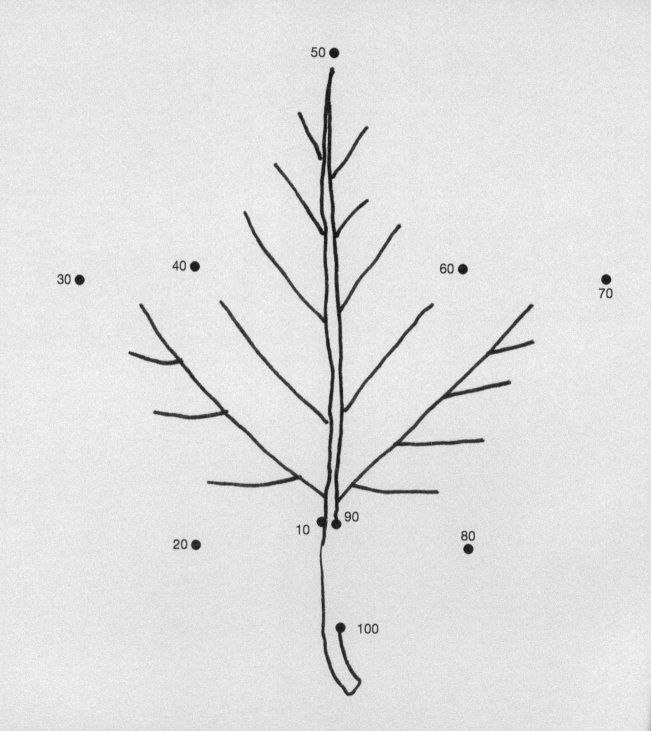

21 22 23 24 25

Draw a picture of something you do in each month.

January	February
March	April
May	June

Trace.

26 27 28 29 30

Draw a picture of something you do in each month.

July	August
September	October
November	December

31   32   33   34   35

Fill in the missing dates.

May

Sunday	Monday	Tuesday	Wednesday	Thursday	Friday	Saturday
			1	2	3	____
5	6	7	8	9	____	11
____	13	14	15	16	17	18
19	20	____	22	23	24	25
26	27	28	29	____	31	

Trace.

36 37 38 39 40

Draw a picture of something you do each day.

Sunday

Monday

Tuesday

Wednesday

Thursday

Friday

Saturday

Trace.

Draw a picture of something you do during each time of day.

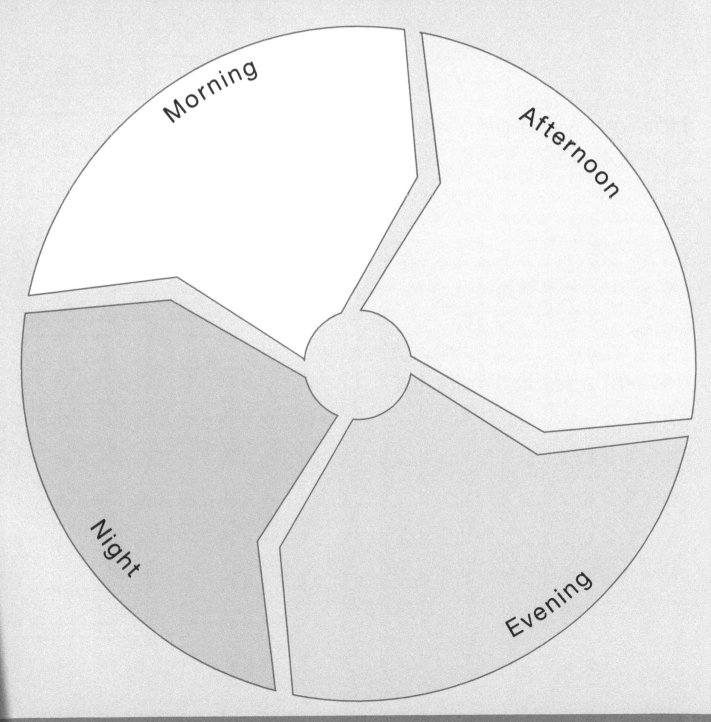

Guess how many times you can do each activity. Then, try it out and write down the actual number.

How many jumping jacks can you do in 1 minute?

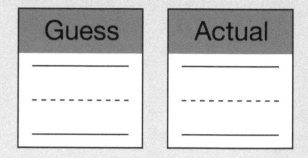

Guess	Actual

How many times can you say the alphabet in 1 minute?

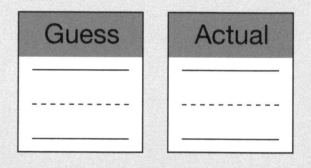

Guess	Actual

How many times can you write your name in 1 minute?

Guess	Actual

51   52   53   54   55

Draw a picture of something you do at each time.

8 o'clock in the morning	3 o'clock in the afternoon
6 o'clock in the evening	**9 o'clock at night**

Trace.

56 57 58 59 60

Match.

4:00	7 o'clock
7:00	12 o'clock
8:00	4 o'clock
12:00	1 o'clock
1:00	5 o'clock
5:00	8 o'clock

Trace.

61 62 63 64 65

Complete.

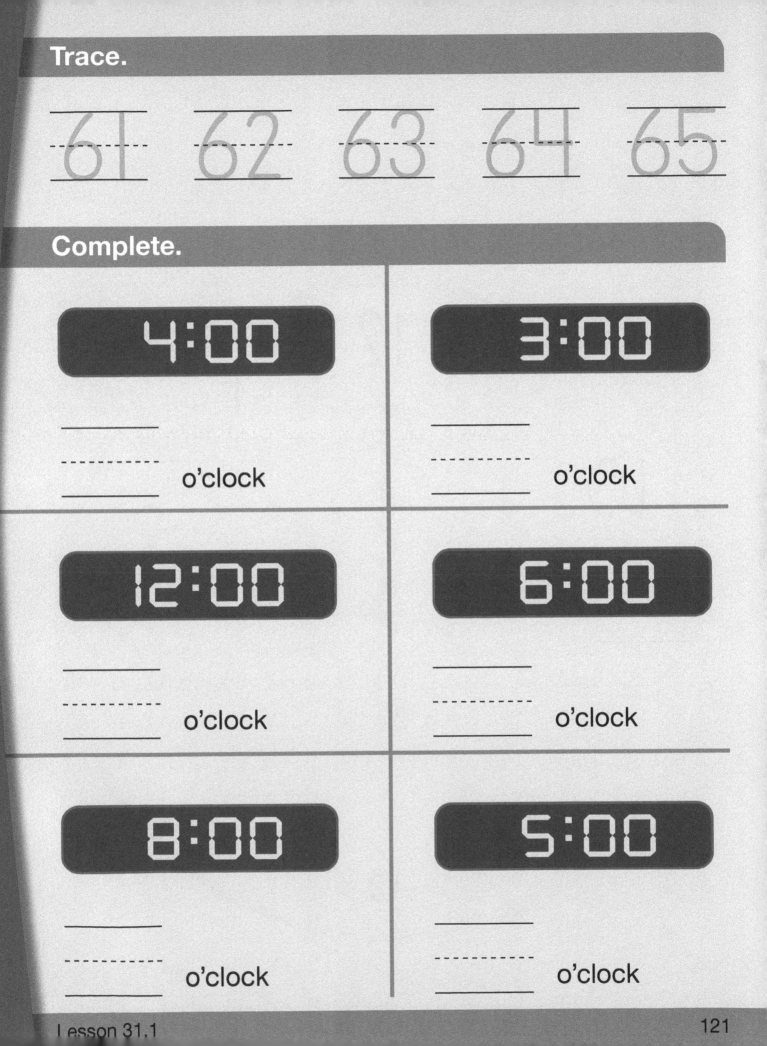

4:00
_____
o'clock

3:00
_____
o'clock

12:00
_____
o'clock

6:00
_____
o'clock

8:00
_____
o'clock

5:00
_____
o'clock

Trace.

66 67 68 69 70

Fill in the missing numbers.

12

1

10

3

7

6

71 72 73 74 75

Complete.

_____ o'clock

_____ o'clock

_____ o'clock

_____ o'clock

_____ o'clock

_____ o'clock

Trace.

76 77 78 79 80

Complete.

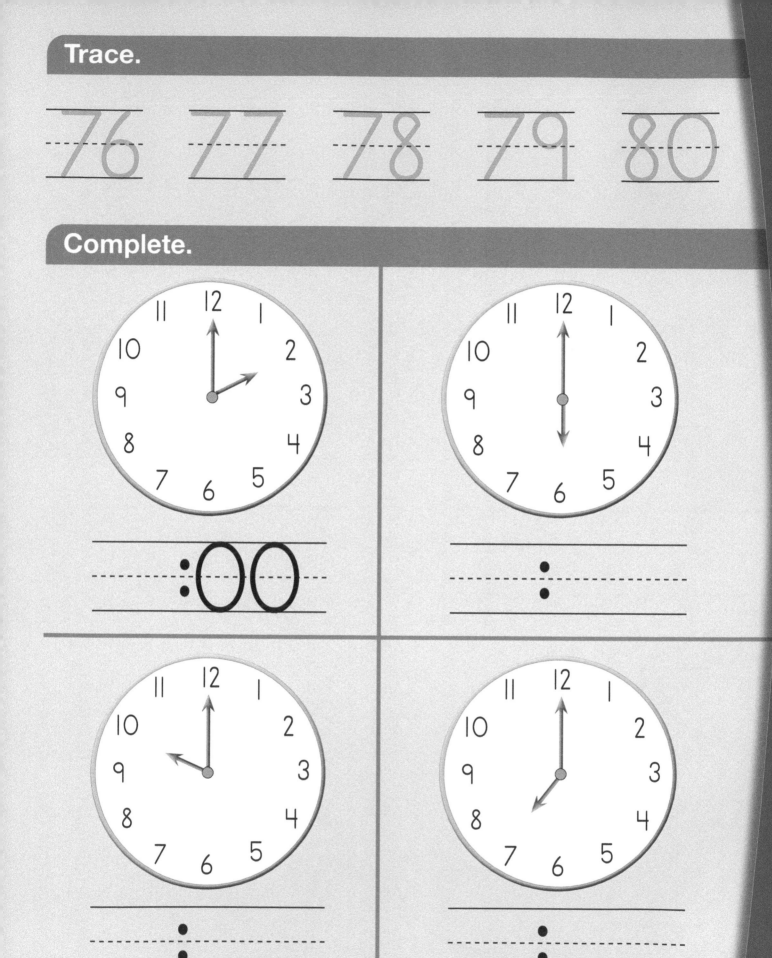

:00

:

:

:

Trace.

81 82 83 84 85

Match pairs that make 10.

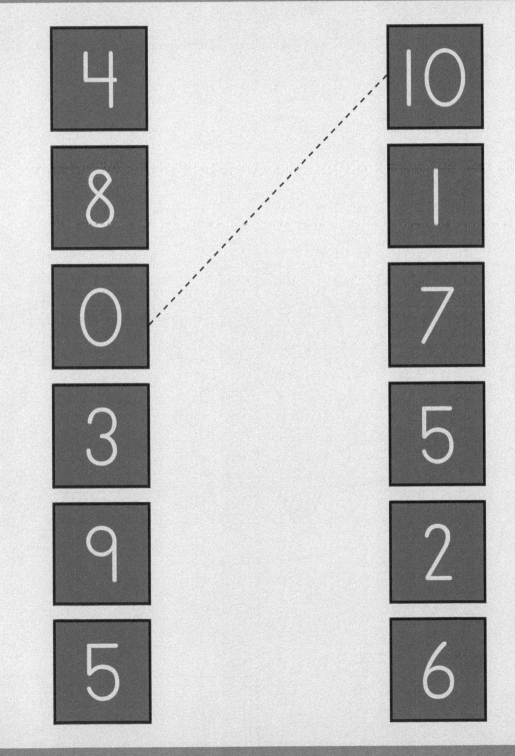

Trace.

86   87   88   89   90

Color the triangles green.
Color the circles red.
Color the rectangles blue.

Trace.

91 92 93 94 95

Connect the dots in order.

Trace.

96 97 98 99 100

My favorite math activity
this year was _____

_____

_____.

The most interesting thing
I learned in math this year
was _____

_____.

I worked hard to learn

_____

_____

_____.

Next year in math, I hope
to learn _____

_____

_____.

128

Lesson 32.4